# Last Chances

by

Allen Takata

Second edition

# Dedicated to

All those who "aspire to be"
And to fathers and sons everywhere

The late Coach Steven Bridgett
who started me in this sport

Coach Sam Wasserstrom for being such
an influence in my formative years.


Special thanks go out to my sister whose diligence
helped me to make the necessary corrections and edits for
this second edition. This newer version is far less
embarrassing of a product and I hope I can finally put this
project in the rear view mirror.

# Forward

I began writing a blog to pass some idle time and to vent my frustration at what swirls around me each day. My most popular entry came from a letter I wrote to my son after one of his wrestling matches. Colin was only 9 and I hadn't given him the letter but thought someone should read it, and so it went up on the blog (It is also included within the book). The response was wonderful and the comments of thanks gave me a satisfaction that I had never felt before. I had shared my emotions to anyone who ventured to read and it had touched their hearts. In turn they had touched mine.

So then I began to write and before I knew it I was writing "Last Chances". It's my first attempt at doing anything like this and upon editing and rereading, I knew it could be much better. When doing something like this for the first time you begin to recognize the missteps and things that you should have done. But like one of the characters in the book, the only thing I could do was to just keep going forward. Edit after edit and finally I am here.

In truth my writing is much like my wrestling. The more I do it, the better I hope to become. I am not certain how good I am at either endeavor, but I feel I will have my moments of quality from time to time. I hope you can focus on those moments when reading.

Wrestlers feel passionate about their craft. I suppose it is the same for many sports and their athletes. But wrestling is different, just ask any wrestler. People become swallowed by its appeal and the sport becomes central to the person's identity. If you were to sit some of my friends into a psychiatrist's chair and ask them about "who they are", their answer may well be; father, son, husband….wrestler. The word will come up. It may be the first or it might be farther down the line in his personal description, but "wrestler" will certainly be quickly included.

The appeal of wrestling, I think, is its honesty. There is something supremely genuine about a sport that pits one against another in combat. There is nobility in those who endure the training that is required to excel. There is a courage required by those who endure, and brotherhoods shared for all who do.

# The Wrestling Room

Walk into the room and you immediately understand the amount of work being done within it. Not by anything that you see initially, but just the feeling of heat and humidity that hits you as you cross the threshold. The windows are fogged and there seems to be a mist floating in the air as thick as a summer in Southern Mississippi. There is condensation on the walls and pools of sweat can be found all around the mat. Upon further examination, you see combatants who have the look of threatening dangerous men, not pimple faced teens who beg for the car on a Saturday night. Eyes are focused, muscles are straining, and there is struggle and anguish with each movement. It's remarkable to realize that three hours ago these menacing warriors were struggling over the Pythagorean Theorem or explaining why their History assignment wasn't completed.

Battles continue around the room as wrestlers shout and push each other beyond what most people can even imagine let alone actually experience. The ages range from fourteen to eighteen. Some are still looking for their first real date while one team member has just recently become a father. There are young men of gargantuan strength and fierceness side by side with utter children. But, because they all share the same pain, the same desire, the same goals, they also share the same respect and the same bond. They comprehend something that other athletes will never understand. They understand the grueling aspects of a sport that is misjudged and underappreciated. They recognize the discipline and share in the sacrifice of struggling through that pain in virtually anonymity. They know what it is to be a wrestler.

Wrestling is almost cult-like when compared to

other sports in high school, or anywhere else for that matter. Football and basketball are kings while wrestling teams are relegated to practicing on stages or basements or hallways or even balconies. On any October Friday night, high school stadium stands are filled with students, alumni, teachers, and local fans not even associated with the school, to watch high school football. They will cheer and sit through frigid temperatures, rain and wind. Yet, in February, the stands are empty in most gyms during a wrestling meet. You would be hard pressed to find anyone in the stands at a wrestling tournament who is not a family member of a wrestler. Wrestling fans are either former wrestlers or related to a wrestler. You almost have to be drafted or born into the sport.

However, the young men struggling through another practice today couldn't care less about any of that. Their focus right now is merely to survive the last half hour of today's session of torture. Fatigue is more the enemy than the wrestler across from them. Pride drives each individual. There is no room for cowards on this team. Coaches scan the room looking for the next wrestler that needs a push. Who needs to be called out to prevent him from giving in to the fatigue that would make most succumb? Captains try to set the example, freshmen try to keep up and prove their worth. Tendons and ligaments strain to survive the twists and stretching that is all so very common.

Jake is in command of his opponent, as is usually the case. As a sophomore, he is one of two underclassmen who are the future of this program. Today is not unlike all the other practices he's been through. For the past nine years, he's been rolling on wrestling mats and performing the moves and drills he practices today. Repetition mixed with intensity is a winning combination. Jake also has a desire that is not matched by many others in the sport. To be involved in wrestling requires a commitment like no other venture, but to excel in it, is a completely different animal. If you ask Jake where he got that desire, that drive, to become a state champion, he'd look at you with a tilt of his head and have to try to first understand the strange question before coming up with an answer. Even then, he could not provide a real reason for his desire. It's just something that he grew up with. His dad is a wrestler and has coached him since he was small, just as he continues to coach him to this day. The goal of becoming a state champion was something as common as waking every morning and running before breakfast. It was natural, as if everyone in the world had the same ambition. To not have that drive was foreign to Jake, and to his family.

For some, it might be difficult to have your father as your high school coach but for Jake it's natural. It's all he'd ever known. He's never had another coach and to have anyone but his father would make the experience completely different, it just wouldn't be the same sport. It's so central to their relationship that even on Father's Day the card will read, "I love you Coach".

Jake's dad blows a whistle and shouts out, "Last 6 minutes!" This meant that the last session of live wrestling was about to start and everyone had to find a tough opponent to finish the practice off with. The toughest challenge is saved for the toughest six minutes of the practice. For Jake it was his best friend, and without any words or even acknowledgement, Spencer Howard lines up across from the coach's son just as they have done so many matches, so many periods, so many times before.

Spencer Howard is also a sophomore and is the other half the duo that will define the program for the next three years. They started the sport together and have been going through the same ritual for almost a decade. They've shaped each other into the athletes they are today, and know that much of their future success will also depend on their greatest asset, each other. *As iron sharpens iron, so one man sharpens another." Proverb 27:17*

Six minutes later the whistle blows and they both roll to their backs in exhaustion. They each take a breath, get right back to their feet, and get ready, because practice still has one final ingredient, conditioning. It's a series of drills at the end of practice and is yet another situation when a wrestler battles between his physical fatigue and his mental resolve. It's not just about becoming physically superior but to become mentally stronger. It's because of these moments that wrestlers painfully endure each day that tell them they are stronger, tougher, and have more heart than the next guy. It puts a chip squarely on their shoulder and dares anyone to knock it off. Yes, the sport is different. It's not understood, it's not appreciated, for many schools it's almost ignored, and those reasons alone make it special and the pursuit of excellence within it becomes unique, courageous…even noble.

Captains shout and coaches call out the next drill and then the next and the next. Sounds of heavy breaths, groans of struggle, and feet pounding the mat fill the room as the captains direct. The team counts their repetitions with the precision of a platoon of marines. When pride begins to falter to fatigue and endurance begins to wane, it only takes the teammate next to you to tell you to keep pushing. That's enough to get you through because you know that you're all in it together and you're not alone in the struggle. Endurance builds, character fosters, determination is cemented, and men are created.

The last drill is completed and the team begins to clap in unison. Shirts are soaked with sweat, the eyes of many seem to be empty, and expressions are emotionless. Hands clap as one, and they speed, and slow together. Captains gather at the center of the mat as the rest of the team surrounds them as one unit. A few words of encouragement, a joke and some laughs are allowed as the intensity subsides. Each practice has drawn them closer and closer together. Most of the coaches disappear into the locker room because the team is functioning on all cylinders now and the final moments of practice today are left for the captains, and the rest of their surrogate family. After a few minutes, the team separates into three informal groups. One group retires to the locker room to shower and end the day. Another group continues their quest for excellence by adjourning to the weight room. Finally, a small group remains in the wrestling room as if they need just a few more repetitions to reach perfection of a move.

Cars begin to drive through the parking lot to pick up their embattled young men. Tonight there is still dinner and homework that must be dealt with. The wrestlers have a renewed energy as they part each night only to begin again tomorrow. By himself, Spencer Howard jogs the short two miles to his home. Coach Stevens used to drive him but Spence often prefers taking the time to walk or jog it by himself. A light snow begins to fall and every exhale blows white clouds like the smoke stacks of the factories seen in the distance. Jake watches the solitary shadow drift away into the night and smiles with both understanding and admiration. It seems fitting to see his teammate, best friend, one of the best wrestlers in the area, travel alone in the dark. They belong to a wrestling team, but in the final analysis, it is a sport of individuals. Wrestlers each bask in victory or suffer defeat on our own. They are all together, ultimately alone.

The wrestling mat itself, can be a lonely place. Whatever weakness you have can be exposed for all to see. There is no hiding and no teammate to cover it up. A wrestler is alone and teammates are there, not to resolve, but to only share in the solitude. Spencer, however, is even more secluded than most. He comes home to a small empty house while mom waits tables. The house is dark and quiet with only the kitchen light on. There's always a plate of dinner left for him in the fridge, always, every night, consistent and predictable. He'll usually do homework or sometimes not. There are days when he just crashes into his bed and stares to the ceiling. It doesn't take much detective work to recognize that wrestling is the primary activity in this household. The house deco is kind of a "Midwestern grappler" motif. Pictures of Spencer litter the living room and his bedroom displays trophies and medals of successes in years past. There is one picture that is curious and stands apart from all the others.

It's a photo of a lone pair of wrestling shoes, worn and used, resting at the center of a mat. Almost cliché, some wrestlers have been known to leave their shoes on the mat to signify their last match and their exodus from the sport. The shoes in the photo belongs to Jon Trenge who upon winning his NCAA match for third place in the nation, left his shoes on the mat and walked off to tell the crowd that he was done. His hand raised in victory and his journey complete. Although that journey's destination was not a national championship, it was one that demanded admiration and respect. It was also a glaring reminder to Spencer that this sport of wrestling that has identified him for the past nine years, must someday come to an end and that his journey will also, someday be complete. All that remains to be seen is where that journey will ultimately lead.

The photo was only three inches by six but it seemed to be the largest in the room and it spoke volumes to Spencer. It was by far the most important and poignant display on his walls. At 16 years of age, his life would soon meet a crossroads. College was a question mark. Even with scholarship money, it would be hard for his mother to manage it. College scholarships for football seem to flow like Mississippi floodwaters. There are football programs in just about every college and university, big or small. An NCAA 1A school can carry 85 scholarship players and a 1AA school can have 63 players on scholarship. Counting all the scholarships from the 117

1A, 124 1AA, and the 150 division 2 schools, this adds to about 23,000 football scholarships available from the NCAA. Wrestling is very different in its ability to provide money for school. In contrast to football, there are only about 85 Division I schools and 39 Division II schools that have wrestling programs. This number seems to be dwindling each season. This amounts to about 1200 scholarships available for the nation's wrestlers. However, programs have the ability to divide up the money and provide partial scholarships. This way, more athletes can get some money but fewer are able to get a full ride. For the wrestler who absolutely needs every penny in order to survive the costs of college, a partial scholarship might not be enough.

For Spencer this seemed to be the case and he has known it ever since he was in eighth grade. No one in his family ever went to college and even though his mother hopes he'd be able to go, neither one of them has figured out a way to swing it. He's always seen his senior year as the end of the line and every night he looks at that picture of Jon Trenge's shoes as if he needed another reminder that his time is running out.

He feels good about where he is though. He's right on schedule and he's right along side Jake who's been with him since this whole thing started. Last season the two freshmen made the other wrestlers in the state sit up and take notice with Jake placing third and Spencer taking a fourth in their weight classes. Both are favorites to be in the finals this year and, some believe, are good bets to take the state title. Three time state champions are good bets to get those few and precious full rides but he's not banking on any of it. For years, he's been telling himself that his high school career is most likely his only wrestling career. To think beyond that would be a dangerous optimism. Besides, he doesn't wrestle as a path to higher education. He wrestles because, well, he's a wrestler. There's no other way to really put it. When it's all over he knows he'll miss it. Maybe he'll coach or wrestle some open tournaments. He knows that the numbers of competitive seasons are limited and he just might be approaching the end of that limit.

Tonight he'll fall asleep without homework completed and his mother will arrive soon after Spencer has retired on the couch. Janice Howard will smile and throw a blanket over her child just as she did when he was still sleeping in the crib. Life is simple and they've learned to appreciate all they have rather than regret all that they have lost and once had before.

Even with the ease that Jake handles being "the coach's son", being the son of a coach brings about its own set of expectations. When your dad's your coach it's as if you are representing your father and you hold a responsibility to win for your dad. Isn't your skill and toughness a direct reflection of your father's? When you fail isn't that also the failure of your father's ability to lead, to train, to teach, to parent? It's one thing to disappoint your coach, but when your coach is your father it can be unbearable. On the other hand, to win with your father at your side, to feel the pride of your father's embrace as he picks you up in victory celebrating for you as a father, and with you as a coach, is a sensation that few people have experienced and fewer moments can ever duplicate. When your dad is your coach, you share in the pain, the struggle, the heartache as well as in the triumph.

The price to pay for such an opportunity is that you're sometimes trapped. While some kids will find a safe haven, away from parents' rule, at school, when your dad is your coach and a teacher, there is no escape. You feel the presence of your home life in every corner of the school. It might become harder to be just one of the guys. A cloud might follow you through the halls and an umbilical chord is attached to you as everything you do is watched, or at least it would seem so. During practices, you follow the same routine and if anyone walked into the room no one would ever guess that you're any different than any of the other forty or so sweaty bodies in the room. You don't take the lead, never shout or yell, and let the coaches and the captains make the noise in the room. Jake is a leader but right now he's one of the quieter ones.

Although grades are important in the Stevens' household, they still take a bit of a backseat to wrestling during the winter months. In the years to come, David and Sarah Stevens see their oldest son going to college somewhere nearby. They are both educated and expect nothing less for their two sons. Also on the slate are a couple of state titles for Jake as well as his young brother James, who just began his career at the tender age of eight, although it can be considered by some to be a late start. A wrestling scholarship is expected in the future but regardless of what happens in Jake's wrestling career, he will be going to school somewhere, wrestling or not. They've both planned for all of this many years ago as a young married couple just out of college. They envisioned their lives just as they are living it today.

Dinner at the Stevens home is social with the four of them sitting around the table talking about the day's events. The conversations often centers on the sport but will also divert to what young James learned today and he happily parrots off some facts about History or Science. Sarah discusses plans for the summer and will likely prod Jake to eat more dinner even though he needs to maintain his weight. The coach at the table will not say too much about Jake's eating habits. He knows Jake understands what he needs to do and he knows that complaining about a son's eating habits is a wrestling mother's right. Besides, it's one of the predictable and amusing aspects of the nightly family dinner.

David and Sarah met in college during their senior year as David was competing to be a two time All-American. He looks much the same as he did 20 years ago. His forearms look larger than his biceps and his face chiseled and lean. His hard squared jaw line and puffed cauliflower ears give away his past. Although James still calls him dad there will come a time when he'll call him "Coach" just the way Jake does. Coach Stevens is well known in wrestling circles not for just being a fine coach but for being one of the most affable coaches around. On the side of the mat you might see some coaches yell and scream over a bad call, but not Stevens. When a wrestler comes off the mat there is always a handshake and congratulations for the effort, even if the effort is not what he had hoped for. Positive and energized is the way to describe the coach. It sometimes seems amazing to Sarah when she witnesses the energy her husband has. She smiles whenever she watches David roll with young James in the living room and it warms her beyond description thinking about how close this sport has made David and Jake. Marrying your college sweetheart with two great kids, Sarah has all she had hoped for, but sometimes happy endings arrive too soon and twist within its fate.

## Sophomore Regionals

Saturday mornings start early as the sun isn't quite peaking over the horizon and muscles aren't quite ready to pull off the covers and begin the long day. Saturday is tournament day. Parents pack the car with; water, sandwiches, apples, oranges, bananas, Gatorade and whatever else will sustain their young wrestler through the next 12 hours or so. The sun begins to peer through the curtains as Jake checks his weight and spits. After brushing his teeth, a stick of gum goes right into his mouth. He'll spit into a cup all the way to the tournament to assure he makes his weight. He takes a small sip of water to briefly satisfy his dry throat. On the ride, Jake hardly talks as he leans against the window trying to catch a few more minutes of sleep. It's about an hour drive to the Regional tournament that will decide who will continue on to the final state tournament.

Spencer is waiting outside his house and hops in the backseat without much more than a quiet good morning. He looks at Jake, nods at the spit cup, and asks how much? Jake responds, "I'm right on", meaning that he is right at his desired weight to wrestle today. Spencer looks back at his house thinking about how tired his mother has looked as she comes home these past few nights. By the time the tournament ends, she'll be back at work without seeing her son for a single moment on this Saturday. Looking into the front seat and seeing Coach and Mrs. Stevens about to spend the entire day with their oldest son gives him a sense of envy, and a sadness that he has to fight off from time to time. It's hard to take pride in being a top athlete, pursuing a state title, spending hours upon hours practicing and conditioning, while watching all the sacrifices made at home. At 16, an age that lies somewhere between man and child, Spence thinks about the selfishness in his personal quest to be the best. The guilt that he carries with him will sometimes rise to the surface especially when he spends time with Jake and his family.

The stands are filled with wrestlers, parents, siblings and girlfriends. Jake's first match is with a cross-town rival from Baker H.S. Dean Atkins is a muscle bound hot tempered senior with a very real mean streak. Jake beat him earlier in the season by a technical fall, the equivalent of the slaughter rule in little league baseball, and Atkins didn't take the embarrassment very well. After the match, he refused to shake Jake's hand and went chest to chest almost starting a melee during the dual meet. Dean Atkins has tattoos going up and down his left leg and his right shoulder blade. He has a crazy look in his wide-open eyes and seems like he is always ready to hit someone. He looks like he belongs to the local correctional facility more than he does a high school class. Today he is wired and ready to wrestle, fight, injure, whatever. Many people believe that the Baker program is dirty and Atkins is one of the reasons.

Depending on the article or the study, it's estimated that 3% - 6% of high school athletes have used steroids. Atkins' strength, aggression, and his penchant for slamming his opponent to the mat was a clear indicator, to many, that something was not right with his training methods, but who could ever say for sure? No one wants to be the one to point the accusing finger; no wrestler ever wants to be the one who makes excuses for losing.

The first period opens with Atkins being aggressive and trying to muscle and bully. He takes control, grabs Jake by the back of the neck, and jerks him up and down. It's more of an attempt to intimidate than it is to score. Coach Stevens calls out, "Stay out of the tie!" Jake needs to attack the legs and shoot (lunging for your opponent's legs) from the outside instead of letting Atkins use his strength to muscle and wear him down. The game plan is to circle and have Atkins chase, keeping him off balance and frustrated just like in their match earlier this season. The last thing Coach wants is to let Atkins grab Jake by the back of the neck and move him around.

But instead of avoiding the tie up, Jake uses it to his advantage and hooks Atkins' upper arm while stepping off to the side. Jake pulls Atkins hand off his neck and slips around Atkins' own momentum. Takedown Stevens; and Jake lets him go and goes back to work to take him down again. This time he stays away and fakes an attack to the legs, slaps Atkins' head, then circles left and lunges to the right. He attacks low and Atkins falls to the mat as if he reached for Jake only to find the wind left behind him. Another two points takes the match to 4-1. Expecting Jake to let him go again Atkins relaxes for a second, and to let one of the elite wrestlers in the state feel that pause will cost you every time. Quickly, Jake turns Atkins just enough to expose Atkins' back to tilt toward the mat for two more quick points. It's 6-1 as the first period ends. Jake looks over to his coach with confidence but Coach Stevens is too tense and knows anything can happen in a match when your opponent is as strong and unpredictable as Atkins. The coach peers back at Jake with intensity to let Jake know that it's nowhere near over.

Spencer is on the next mat with Assistant Coach Davis in his corner. He's making quick work of his opponent and scores methodically. He will move on to the next round without much trouble. During his match, he glances over to Jake's mat and smiles when he sees the score. It's all pretty much as expected. Near the end of the third period as Spencer is finishing his workman-like performance, he hears the sound that you don't normally hear at a wrestling match. The sound of impact that's so loud that it's clear that something is wrong. A section of the crowd gasps and in a second, all eyes fall on Jake

Stevens, writhing on the mat in pain. Slam! Atkins had picked up Jake and, instead of returning him to the ground safely as the rules state, Jake was forcefully bounced to the mat.

Coach Stevens kneels next to his son while the crowd is yelling and calling for a disqualification. Jake sits up and nods his head in assurance to his coach. The score is now 10-4 with Jake winning handily. If he cannot continue, the match will be his with Atkins losing by disqualification because of the illegal maneuver. With so much at stake and an opponent with nothing to lose, the smart move is to stay on the mat and take the win by DQ. It's the smart move but not the honorable one, even with a big lead. When you come to wrestle, you wrestle. Jake stands up and the crowd applauds to show their appreciation for his toughness. Coach Stevens has some words for the ref, as well as for the Baker coach. Coach Jones, the Baker coach, just throws his hands and looks away. His father's only words for Jake is to, "Wrestle smart, one minute left. Win and move on." The message is clear. Atkins means nothing. Jake needs to think beyond this one match and this one wrestler.

Jake understands but the adrenaline is rushing through him. Spencer has his hands raised in victory and then runs to Jake's mat, "Get 'em Jake!" Coach tells Spence to shut up and turns to Jake again and warns him to wrestle smart. Emotions are running a bit too high though and Jake clubs Atkins on the side of the head, fakes a shot, and clubs him again. The ref stops the match and talks to both wrestlers. He knows what he has on his hands and only wants the better wrestler to win.

When the action begins again, Jake takes Atkins down and just as quickly lets him up again. Atkins charges hard, like a bull in a steroid rage, and Jake hooks an arm and launches Atkins with a perfect throw straight to his back, pin. There is to be no stalling, no running, and no protecting a lead. Jake wanted to go head to head and chest to chest with no backing down.....on to the next round.

Both Jake and Spencer rest in the stands as they await the final round. On the mat the consolation rounds are in process, as wrestlers vie for the right to wrestle for third place and go on to the state meet. Losers will have to wait for next season and if you're a senior, well, your wrestling career becomes something to look back upon, because you've reached the end of the line. Parents and coaches feel the brunt of this round as they see their sons and athletes fall one by one. Each mat has a wrestler who goes on and one that goes home. This is the blood round.

Looking onto mat one you see evidence of what this round is all about and both Jake and Spencer are watching this one closely. John Kim wrestled with both boys as a youth until John's family moved away five years ago. They would see each other during the summer tournaments and at all the big tournaments during the season. They all remember going camping with their dads as kids, and the burgers and ice cream after Sunday youth tournaments. John is a sophomore and a win will take him to the third place match at 160 pounds. He's wrestling Vance Tolliver who took second place at the state tournament the past two years and this was going to be the year he made it to the top. Struggling with a shoulder injury he lost in an upset earlier today and another loss will dash all hopes of a state title and end his high school career.

John is quick and confident, and this is a chance to take out the potential state champ before they even get to the tournament. Vance knows that it's now or never and he can't determine if he feels desperation, or fear, as John Kim takes him down and also takes a two point lead. Vance escapes and looks over to his coach, he hears his father's voice shout from somewhere in the gym and in his mind he sees his mother in the stands yelling and crying all at the same time. Takedown Kim, escape Tolliver, takedown Tolliver, escape Kim. The match goes back and forth like a tennis volley. Down by a point and only thirty seconds left on the clock, Vance feels the eyes of the crowd vigilantly anticipating an upset and his elimination. Everyone is watching this one now and he feels the electricity, he feels the adrenaline, he feels the urgency, but he also feels the end at hand. A takedown wins it but he doesn't have much time and Kim will stall and stay away from any sort of attack. Kim circles, fakes and plays defense. A final desperate shot by Vance and the ref blows the whistle as time runs out on the match along with Vance Tolliver's hopes of what has eluded him again, only this time there are no more chances, no more next years. He has run out of time and run out of seasons.

As Jake and Spencer cheer for their friend, their eyes are not on John as his hand is raised. Their eyes, as well as all the eyes in the gymnasium, are on Vance Tolliver. They watch with sympathy, and curiosity, at the reactions of a fellow wrestler having wrestled his last match. As the crowd around them cheer for John Kim, Spence and Jake both stop clapping and stare in silence as Tolliver slowly shakes the hand of Kim and his coach. Vance keeps his head down as sweat streams off his face that serve to hide the tears that also fall to the mat. Vance hugs his coach and this body seems to collapse within the embrace. Mrs. Tolliver cries into the shoulder of her husband as Mr. Tolliver chokes back tears of his own. He is filled with both pride and sorrow, as he watches his son walk off the mat for a final time. Vance will go into the record books as 6th – 2nd – 2nd and DNQ, did not qualify. Without a word, Spence, Jake and Coach Stevens stand and begin to applaud again, but this time not for the wrestler moving on but for the wrestler who is going home.

Amidst all the drama, the coaches have to move

from their seats because Rich Tado, their 215 pound senior is up facing his last chance at becoming a state qualifier. Jake, Spence and Tommy, the team captain, go over and give Rich a handshake and a slap on the back, "Your turn! It's your turn T-man". Rich is one of the athletes that got into the sport late in life, joining only during his sophomore year. One of the hardest workers on the team, Rich has made the most out of the short amount of time he's had in the sport. He faces a wrestler who has been wrestling since 5th grade and just barely weighs over 200 pounds. In between weight classes, Dave Elias is stuck facing wrestlers 10 -15 lbs. heavier. Looking at the two together, you'd never guess that Elias is the lighter of the two as his muscularity makes him an imposing figure.

Elias starts out fast with a high crotch takedown. Tado struggles and cannot escape but is able to fight off every attempt to turn him to his back. Elias throws in a leg and it looks like he'll ride out for the rest of the period. Just before time expires, Rich hits a roll for a reversal. Both on their feet for period two, Elias tries a throw and is countered to his back. The score becomes 7-2 and Tado looks like he'll be going to the tournament that has eluded him the past three years. A scramble for a takedown ends up with Rich briefly exposing his back to the mat and in that split second, that one little mistake, and Elias takes advantage and suddenly Rich Tado is looking up at the lights of the gymnasium. Panic comes quickly when you're on your back and you search for the strength that will save you. You wiggle, squirm, and try to find any angle you can to keep one shoulder off the mat. Back and forth you search for space and then you hear it. The ref slaps the mat and the whistle blows. In the papers tomorrow it will only show that Dave Elias defeated Rich Tado by fall. There will be no mention of Tado in charge for much of the match or that he was only one and half minutes from victory. There will be no mention of the hours of dedication and the strides made by a three-year wrestler. There will be no description of the tears, and the pain, that followed this match. There will be no account of how he fell in love with a sport that will identify him for the rest of his life, after only three short seasons. There will be no picture of a wrestler sitting alone on the floor in a corner of a locker room or reference of the shame he feels walking off the mat. It will only say D. Elias win by fall.

There are two mats set up for the finals. On one mat the Regional champion will be decided and the loser of that match will be the second best wrestler in a region of thirty high schools. The mat next to it will be for third place but all four wrestlers will be moving on to the big tournament in two weeks. For some in the gym today just reaching the state tournament has been the goal but for others the expectations are far greater. Coach Stevens has three wrestlers vying for first place today. Along with Jake and Spencer, Tom Chernich is also looking for a Regional championship. Another wrestler going for a third place, senior Dave Ross has extended his wrestling career for another two weeks. Now, after so many moments of emotional highs and lows, after so many hours of wrestling, waiting, and wondering, the day is coming to its conclusion. And like it has been all day long there will be elation and disappointment, conquests and the conquered.

The team sits around a table amass with food and drink brought by parents. Teammates who are out of the tournament have recovered from disappointment and have reverted to the personalities of high school teenagers. Dressed in street cloths they joke and kid with those that are about to wrestle in the finals. Some wrestlers call girlfriends on the phone, parents chat with each other and coaches take a few moments to gobble a quick meal. Tom Chernich is the lone wrestler missing from the festivities. Tommy will be the first of the remaining wrestlers to have his fate played out. At 189 pounds he is a mass of strength and ripped muscle. His short-cropped blonde hair, squared jaw, and mat burns on his cheekbones display the look of a wrestler. He paces alone, up and down a dark secluded hallway with earphones to shut out any distractions. The setting sun beaming through the windows casts an orange glow at his feet as Tommy prepares much like a warrior prepares for battle. Alone and in silence, he wrestles the match in his mind like a fighter shadow boxing in an empty ring. He wrestles the match right there in the hall. His body moves and plays out the shots and the escapes, rehearsing for the real show to come.

Coach and Jake sit with mom for a while. Sarah asks Jake how he feels and gives him a hug and kisses his cheek. They sit as a family as they have countless other times over the years. Spence and John Kim come over and sit with the Stevens' family. Not much has changed since those days when Jake, Spence and John were playing tag in the hallway in between matches. For a moment each one of them think back to those days and look at each other pleased to where they have arrived.

Tommy warms up in a corner of the gym as his opponent eyes him from the other side of their mat. The boys walk over and Spencer slaps Tommy on the back and pumps him up, "You Ready?" He then gives a slap to each side of Tommy's head. "Let's go killer!"

Spence, like Jake, is a quiet leader in the practice room can't help but to pump up not only for his own match but for his wrestling brother as well. Even though his family at home is limited to just his mother, his family at school is a team of forty-five strong. With that, Tommy runs to the corner of the mat where his coach is waiting with few instructions, "Set up your shot, be patient." Tommy just nods and heads to the center circle.

Like he has so many times this season Tommy ignores anything his coach has said and charges hard and takes an immediate shot and gets a quick takedown. Like a bully in a playground he begins to maul his opponent.

Coach Stevens just smiles and shakes his head as Asst. Coach Davis cheers next to him. Tom is the most physical wrestler on the team and there is nothing pretty about his victories. He's a machine that has one gear and one direction, full speed and straight ahead. Tom turns his opponent and begins to squeeze his head like he was waiting to hear the bones in his skull crack. Tommy's face has a grimace that borders on the maniacal and it brings smiles to everyone on his team. Jake and Spencer scream and bang into each other in celebration. A few moments later, Tom Chernich has his hand raised and is a regional champion.

The melodrama continues with cheers and swells of applause rising and subsiding every 6 minutes or so. Each team has their own set of stories both victorious and tragic. Dave Ross and Jake Stevens win without much drama and the last member of the team to step onto the mat is Spencer Howard. Those in the know have been looking forward to this match. It pits the number two and the number four ranked wrestlers in the weight class and this match can be a good indicator of what is to come in two weeks.

Going into the third period it's tied at 4-4 and Spencer has the choice of starting positions and takes the down, or defensive, position. Getting an escape gives him a one point lead and he looks to find an opportunity and bides his time blocking any attempts of Phil Saleh to turn him. Saleh continues to work, Spencer makes the mistake of looking too passive, the referee penalizes Spence for "stalling", and Spence is now losing by a point. With time running out he needs to get away just to stay alive and get to an overtime.

Coach Stevens yells, "Get it going Spence you gotta score!" Looking up at the clock he sees the end approaching as each tick comes closer to "00.00 seconds". Fans strain in their seats and Jake runs up to the edge of the mat as his shouts blend in like a single drop of rain

24

among a thunderous storm. Spence gets his hips out ever so slightly but Saleh is right on top of the action. Spencer moves and Saleh follows. With each maneuver Spence gets a little more space a little more opportunity. Saleh desperately follows each move but he's just trying to catch up to Spence and as the seconds tick you can hear Jake's voice over the rest of the crowd. He's the first to recognize that Spencer has him and Jake jumps, raises his hands, and turns to the crowd. Two points, a reversal just as time runs out earns a victory for Spence. Saleh lies on his back for a split second, which takes an eternity, to completely take in just what has happened and to allow his heart to completely sink into his stomach. The emotions of the moment can be seen everywhere; in the stands where parents hug and cry with both joy and agony, at the mat corners where coaches celebrate and console, and on the mat where Spencer Howard raises his fists to the crowd in victory and Phil Saleh hangs his head, standing alone with his failure.

Coach Stevens has four wrestlers moving on and it's been a great day. Family and friends celebrate as the season continues for four well deserving warriors. Rich Tado sits alone near a corner of the gym and looks over the final proceedings, stone-faced. Sitting near the top of the stands with hands folded and his warm-up covering his head as if to shield himself, he watches in silence as wrestlers stand atop the podium and are given medals. Family members come to the floor to take pictures and he experiences the final moments of his wrestling career as more of a spectator than a participant. His four teammates understand that the regional championship is just another steppingstone in their quest, a goal reached only to pursue the next. But for those like Tado, the journey is over with its conclusion ending too soon.

# Sophomore States

It's almost March, and for most of the country that means college basketball and soon, "March Madness". On this particular Saturday evening UCLA plays Arizona and millions around the country watch to see the outcome of this PAC 10 rivalry. Still others enjoy the approach of warmer weather and plan for the summer and rejoice in the scent of spring. Grass begins to become greener, days become longer, and life becomes sweeter. For others, the final days of February means the state tournament and the culmination of a long grueling season of wrestling. As the cars drive past the stadium today, drivers will look with curiosity as to what could be happening and what event could possibly fill the parking lot. Today is the finals and it's been a hard and disappointing few days for Coach Stevens.

On this occasion, the promise fell far short of performance. Dreams remained blurred in the imagination as hopes were dashed in earlier rounds of the two day tournament. Both Jake and Spence have lost in their semi-final match and are climbing back to salvage a third place. Dave Ross can win his next match but will have to settle for a 5th. Tom Chernich is the only wrestler still vying for a championship and will be the only one on the team to be competing under the spotlights tonight.

Coach Stevens tries desperately to keep his kids upbeat and prepared to finish the season with a victory. It's easy to sense the anti-climactic cloud that covers them as they warm-up for their last match. Coach Stevens has his game-face on in hopes that his wrestlers won't let down. As a team, the four wrestlers and two coaches meet in one corner of the warm-up area. The coaches remind them of the hard work they've put in for the past four months, the hours or training all summer, and of the sacrifices they've made in and out of the wrestling room.

They talk about desire, and commitment and their pursuit of greatness. The four young men stand in silence taking every bit of advice and wisdom. The words of the coaches fill the wrestlers' hearts and fill them with nourishment for their weakening resolve. The young men walk away from the huddle with a different look in their eyes and a new manner in their stride. They are ready for battle and Coach Stevens' has successfully hidden the disappointment that sticks in his throat.

Two hours later and most of the season has completely played itself out. The countless hours of work, the injuries, the sacrifice all come to a merciful, if not subdued, ending. Each wrestler comes to the mat ready to attack. There is no let down until the final whistle blows. At the end of each match, victory is still bitter sweet. Dave Ross wins his last match and comes away with a fifth. Jake and Spencer, both favorites in the eyes of many to take their first state title, win their final match but it's one round short and they both end up two podium steps away from their goal. They will accept their third place medal with a happiness mixed with regret. The stands will applaud and flash bulbs flutter for several moments and the season ends with a whimper that will echo within them all summer long.

The only wrestler Jackson still has in contention is Tommy Chernich. He will have 2 hours to wait for the round to begin. While some wrestlers might lie down and rest, and then possibly take a quick shower in order to be fresh for the big match. Tommy takes the time to eat almost half an apple pie and do some math homework. Tommy's…different.

At 4:00 p.m. the wrestlers, parents, coaches and fans file into the stadium awaiting the beginning ceremony to begin at five. Every few minutes, people glance at their watches in anticipation, and debates over who will be the next state champions are discussed throughout the stands. A beach ball begins to make its rounds through the stands as if the entire wrestling community was spending time at a huge picnic. The five o'clock hour comes and goes and the audience grows impatient and begins to clap in unison, slow and steady like the pulse of a beating heart. At five minutes past the hour, the lights dim and the crowd stands to its collective feet. Spotlights dance throughout the stadium as the PA system sounds with a booming voice welcoming the audience to the spectacle. The "Grand March of Champions" begins with the playing of the Olympic Theme song, "Summon the Heroes". From the far side of the building the athletes begin to emerge from the tunnel. Spotlights follow the wrestlers as they appear and other lights continue to dance through the stands.

Spectators applaud, whistle, and yell with appreciation. Meanwhile, amidst all the electricity, Jake and Spencer stand in silence holding back their own emotions, silent and almost motionless. They clap as if in a trance, they don't comment or even look at each other. The two boys merely stare at the pageantry as the wrestlers file into the stadium, knowing that they should be there and silently vowing that next season they won't be left in the stands, watching. In the same choreographed path the march has taken for as long as anyone can remember, the wrestlers split into two lines and march along opposite ends of the mats. The spotlights stop dancing as the procession stops and now each wrestler faces across the mat to his opponent.

Tommy's weight shifts back and forth. His eyes wander from the crowd, to his opponent, and down to his feet, as he awaits his name to be called, "From Jackson High School, coached by David Stevens, with a record of 43 and 4, Junior, Thomas Chernich". Tommy runs to the center of the mat and a spotlight follows his every step. "From St. Andrew's High School, coached by Steven Bridget, with a record of 45-1, returning state champion at 189 lbs, Nick Carengella"…

There's an emptiness going back to the hallways of school on Monday. Classes seem even more meaningless and the term, "going through the motions", takes on an even a greater definition. There is a feeling that something is missing from the lives of each member of the Jackson wrestling team. With nothing to challenge them, nothing for them to focus upon, with no goal to strive for each day, what is there to do? Some do not even realize they experience this letdown. On the exterior, each wrestler seems to walk the halls with a new expression on their faces. They all seem to be more relaxed and at ease. The invisible grip around their bodies has been taken away, and they are better able to move, better able to breathe. A weight has been lifted and the stress has been removed. But, at the end of the day and the final bell rings, the boys walk past the wrestling room and feel it pulling them back in. The pull is stronger for some than others, but they all feel it to some degree. It's almost like the widower who comes home and in his heart expects to see his departed wife, or the amputee who reaches for the leg that is no longer there.

The annual Spring camping trip is something that the Stevens' boys and Spencer have been doing for years. It's been a tradition that the end of the season brings about a trip to the lake to fish and take a collective breath under the stars. For the last five years, the trip has been without Matthew Howard. The loss of Spencer's dad has made this annual trip even more important to take. All the sprints, lifting sessions, miles of roadwork, military like dedication, and the stress of the season is all put away and the only thing that matters is watching the sun set over the hills and the sound of a line cast out into the water.

It's now been about two months since the disappointment of the state tournament. The boys haven't spoken about it and Coach Stevens makes a conscious effort not to bring it up. The camping trip was put together in order to remedy the situation. It reminds everyone that their lives are more than what happens between November and March. They started this trip back when the two boys were about 6 or 7. The dads would take the boys out for some bonding away from the mat. The kids enjoyed the late night campfires and fishing for trout and now almost a decade later, it is all pretty much the same.

Spencer and Jake take little James to their secret spot where they seem to always get at least a few bites. As they reach the spot James sits between the two other boys and carefully copies each movement. Silence covers the three as they plunk their lines into frigid lake waters. Ripples of each sunken hook echo across the smooth mirrored surface. As the waves of each dropped line meet each other, James looks up at Spencer and pauses before he speaks, not sure if his words should be spoken by a boy his age. But Spencer is a brother and friend all rolled up into one and James breaks the silence. "Are you still sad about it Spence?" Jake is stunned but just as curious about the answer his young brother has asked. Without even looking up Spencer's body freezes for a moment and shrugs his shoulders. "Yeah, I guess. But ain't nothing I can do about it."

Young James looks over to see if Jake is mad and his older brother only gives a small smile and looks away. James had no idea how big that question was. As they sit in the renewed silence Jake wonders if Spencer's answer was about the tournament or was it about his father. In either case his answer would have been the same. Six years after losing his dad to cancer and Spence still doesn't talk about it much. When you're 10 and you see your father whither away and die, well, it's something that will always stay with you. It'll always be a part of you. The memories of fishing and wrestling, and laughing at the dinner table compete for space in your memory along with the visions of him sick, thin and weakened. The memory of him saying he loved you, and to be good for your mother will always be vivid and haunting. Spencer remembers his dad coaching him as a child, and lifting him up on his shoulders and spinning him in circles. He remembers leaping into his arms after winning his first tournament as a youth. He remembers the pride and love on his father's face when he embraced him at that moment. He also remembers seeing his father lying in his hospital bed too weak to repeat that same embrace, his voice soft and his skin ashen and gray. When your father, your idol, dies, well, how do you recover from something like that? Does the pain stay with you forever? "Yeah, I guess. But ain't nothing I can do about it."

"Jake, what if we don't win it? What if we do a Tolliver and never make it to the top step? It could happen." Jake just looks at him as if he's crazy, then turns away and stares at his fishing line. Most wrestlers walk onto a mat and size up the competition. Does the guy look soft, strong, or tough? Sometimes you run into some tattooed muscle bound beast that looks like he took steroids with his mother's milk when he was a baby. Some kids will lose a match before it even starts just out of being intimidated. But for the better wrestlers the only fear that can be enabling is the fear of failure and Spencer is showing how some of that fear has crept within him.
"Shut up – that ain't gonna happen to us." Was this denial or self-confidence? It doesn't really matter which, as long as he really believes it. The sad truth is that it happens all the time. There are plenty of wrestlers out there that were good enough to take a state title but never did. Injuries, illness, bad calls, one slip, one split second late, one opportunity lost can be the difference between victory and defeat. One loss at the tournament and you're looking up at the top step of the podium. The past season

was a clear indicator of how unexpected results can befall even the best athletes.

Spencer understands the limits of time. He fully understands how every moment needs to be appreciated because it can all pass in the snap of a finger, and everything you once knew to be true can change in that instant. One moment you can be hearing your father at the side of your mat and the next thing you know your dinner table is forever missing a place setting. The future is not something you can take for granted. Outcomes can never be predicted and life itself is fragile and mysterious.

On the ride back home from the camping weekend the two boys take turns with a magic marker. As little James makes the mistake of falling asleep in between the two high schoolers, his young innocent face grows a black inked mustache, then a beard, then a few teardrops and finally some freckles. They hold back the laughter and pass the marker back and forth trying to outdo the other. James flinches and scratches his face as the older boys complete their masterpiece. The little grin on James' face makes the whole thing all the more hilarious. It's tough to be the little one in this group. You have to be able to take some abuse and you have to be on the ball. James learned long ago to expect stuff like this.

He also learned that his brother and Spencer don't pay much attention to him when it's time to pack the tents and it's really easy to stick items into their backpacks without anyone noticing. James will go to bed never noticing the drawings on his face. He'll lie in bed, grinning, totally unaware. He will wake up with that same grin on his face when he hears Jake scream when he discovers the snake in his backpack.

"AAAAAAAAAHHHH!! Jake falls backward and rolls off his bed and thuds onto the floor. "Mom! James put a snake in my bag!!!"

Having no energy to deal with the pranks of her

boys, Sarah Stevens has a suitable response. "That's nice honey. Toss it in the yard and go to bed."

It's just a shame that James can't hear Spencer's reaction to finding the same surprise left for him. Oh well, bedtime, it's good to have brothers.

Coach Stevens is happy to see that things are getting back to normal after the disappointment of states, or at least close to normal. The school year will finish out and the State tournament will be a distant memory. For Tom Chernich it will mark a state championship and for others it will be a haunting reminder. The team will go through summer workouts and go to a wrestling camp or two. Others on the team will wrestle freestyle or Greco-roman tournaments and test their skill against talent from others states. For each one of those summer days there will be a faint, but ever present, ghost of the last state tournament that will shadow both Jake and Spencer.

Jake and Spence spend their summer hitting several tournaments and a camp here and there. There will be few days that wrestling or training isn't a part of the routine. Both boys know that the road to next season began the day after the state tournament. There has never been an "off-season" for them. Each year is filled with either competition or preparation.

# Social Classes

The first matches of the new season starts with a bang. St. Joseph academy is a school a few towns away and just a 30 minutes drive. At the same time, it is worlds apart from what most people know and experience. St. Joseph is a private school in every notion of the term. Every stereotype of the wealthy is clearly represented within its walls. The pampered, self-indulgent, and spoiled, fill the halls with the confidence that only a robust sense of self importance can produce. These young men know only what they have learned from their privileged but sheltered lives. Each will look you in the eye and give you a good firm handshake as if to challenge your masculinity. Somewhere, at some time, fathers have taught them that this was an important measure of a man. Their shirts are clean and pressed, without a thread out of place, or a pleat that is less than crisp.

Andrew Peterson's father is an attorney; his step father is also an attorney. His plans are to become a physician and he's had no other ambition ever since his mother informed him of his goal at the age of 6 years old. Mom often drinks too much red wine and spends her days at the country club. On Sunday brunches, she is sure to wear some of her good jewelry to assure her place in the inner pecking order of the Stratford Country Club. She considers herself a humanitarian every time she donates bags of barely worn clothes to the Salvation Army and donates to her church each week. Isn't it wonderful to be able to get close to God and also take a tax deduction all at the same time? She watches Oprah on occasion so she learns of, and will subsequently understand, the plight of the disadvantaged, and she feels close to the world through her book clubs. She exercises for several hours each day and makes certain that Andrew is on track for

Med-School and a surgical specialty. Life is very busy.

Andrew took up wrestling in high school because he wanted to have a varsity letter on his college applications and he was too small and too uncoordinated for much else. Wrestling was a no cut sport so it was a logical fit. At the tender age of 17 he has more self esteem than actual self worth. He will volunteer his wisdom and give advice on life, love, medicine, money, and parenting even though he's only had one girlfriend, and has never held a job. The apple never does fall too far from the tree.

King H.S is also just a few towns away but might as well be on the other side of the galaxy. King is the other side of the spectrum that colors America's national fabric. Poor, disadvantaged, the underclass, whatever the label is doesn't really matter to those who are living it. For the young men on the wrestling team, the sport is a cherished diversion and something to embrace. For some of these wrestlers the sport has become almost a salvation from their everyday lives. Winning becomes a validation of sorts for them. Winning is a confirmation of their worth and an avenue for success where success is hard to come by, and there's a lot that's hard to come by at King H.S. Books, teachers, money, equipment, are all rare commodities but toughness is one thing that is not in short supply on the King team. Whatever they lack in experience, they make up for with intensity. Much of wrestling is about hardship and sacrifice and those are two items that King H.S. has in great supply.

Tony Hardman began wrestling in middle school when his mother was worried about keeping him occupied and off of the streets. The first practice he attended he sulked at the corner of the room because he couldn't beat anyone. He fought and fought but the other guys knew moves and took advantage of the new kid. At one point his frustration resulted in him punching his workout partner, Jake Stevens. Since then Tony has put on 50 pounds of muscle, a tattoo of his initials and another of a dagger piercing a bleeding heart. Jake and Tony will occasionally laugh about that day and, like John Kim, share a respect and friendship that is directly linked to the times they've shared on the mat.

Today, Jackson H.S. and Coach Stevens will host a "quad" where four teams come together and face off against each other. None of the teams will pose much of a challenge to Jackson H.S. but they usually have a few quality kids and it's always a gut check to face off against a physical team like King. For Jake, Spence, and the rest of Coach Stevens' team, it is a warm up for upcoming competition. For Tony, it's something he's been looking forward to for the last three months. He still hears the chants from the stands of the football stadium last September. The game was in the fourth quarter and King had the game well in hand as Tony ran in another touchdown to put them up by 24. Usually, the stands of the losing team will be pretty quiet, but not this time.

"That's alright, that's okay, you will work for us someday" was the cheer. He looked at the St. Joe's cheerleaders laughing and the handful of adults cheering along to the stupid chant of a loser. The second he got home that night, he looked at the wrestling schedule and circled this date.

The teams are warming up in the gym using any area that is available. Armies of wrestlers jog around the perimeter of the gym falling into rhythm with each step and stride like young recruits at boot camp. Their steps thunder in cadence as they circle like vultures hovering their prey. Another squad of wrestlers line up in rows on one side of a mat stretching and exercising to the signals of their captains with a well rehearsed precision. Sharing the same mat is yet another team in similar rows moving with the same exactness. The invisible wall that separates them prevents any single wrestler from even a glance to the enemy side. A glance or stare could imply that there was concern or a lack of confidence or concentration. I don't care what you look like or what you're doing because I know what I am doing, and what I need to do. All you are is the obstacle I am about to overcome, period. Tony however, does look and does stare. Picking out his opponent on the St. Joe's team from across the gym he focuses on the iPod Andrew Peterson wears, Peterson's over-priced $150 wrestling shoes, and the chant he can still hear clearly in his head from those stands just a few week ago.

At the start of the match Tony goes right after Peterson and pushes and bangs. Tony snaps the head down and sinks into a deep double leg and goes right up to his feet lifting Andrew up into the air with no effort. Tony finishes the takedown with enough force to spark the crowd to gasp but not quite enough to bring a slam call from the referee. Tony fists his right hand and throws his forearm hard against the side of Andrew's cheek with the bone catching the bridge of his nose. The St. Joe's coach jumps up to his feet and yells at the referee complaining about the roughness of the match on his wrestler. But wrestling is a rough sport, and those who aren't prepared for the nature of this sport should not venture into it. The ref ignores the coach and walks to the other side of the mat as Tony lets Andrew go and gives up a point allowing him to escape.

This time Tony seeks to lock up and attacks the upper body. It's clear that Tony has a mission and has his opponent completely outclassed. The two wrestlers move about the mat clinched together and in one sudden and beautiful throw, Andrew's feet are lofted off the mat and lands onto his back. As the referee slaps the mat ending the match, Tony stands with disappointment at the ease of the match. There would have been far more satisfaction if Andrew Peterson had been a little tougher and could hang in a bit longer. The plan was to punish and not to just pin. Tony Hardman walks off the mat looking around the gym as if to challenge anyone who was willing, looking for another opportunity to satisfy his need to impose his will over another. On his way off, he flexes and pounds his chest and then points to the St. Joseph crowd. He sits with his team and allows his rage to settle but, clearly, there is still a fury that churns within him. Spencer's eyes take turns as he bounces from watching his teammate wrestle and on Hardman and Peterson on the other mat across the gym. As Hardman walks off and rejoins his team with his eyes blood red and body tense and still pumped with adrenaline, Spence looks over to Jake. Neither knowing how to comment on Tony, they merely shrug their shoulders with a grin.

The match didn't go unnoticed by Coach Stevens. Practice the next day ends with a discussion about self-control.

"There is a difference between aggression and wrestling aggressively, between intensity and violence. From what I saw yesterday, Hardman crossed that line."

The boys sit looking up at their coach, catching their breath and dripping with sweat. Latching on to every word, they take in every bit of wisdom they can, hoping to soak up another piece to the puzzle, in their quest for perfection.

"You don't win anything by wrestling the way Hardman did yesterday. You don't become a winner, you don't become a better wrestler, and you don't become a better man. Hardman lost something within himself yesterday. He lost a little bit of dignity; he lost a bit of his honor. Don't let that happen to you."

David Stevens understands his role as a coach. Part of that is to be a leader and an example. He's spent his life in the sport and understands all the positives that can come from it. Wrestling has been his father, babysitter, and best friend for most of his life. It taught him all the things that his parents had hoped for him. It taught him the meaning of hard work, setting goals, failure and the perseverance to overcome those failures. Wrestling made him strong and honest. Coach Stevens wants that same experience for his sons and all his surrogate sons on the Jackson team.

# A New Year

Junior year is a year where many kids come of age. It's a year of preparation. It's a big year for the college bound as ACT and SAT tests are taken. Courses are available for those who need help in boosting up those test grades and classes take on a renewed importance. For others it's a year when decisions need to be made about alternatives to college and figuring out what exactly is going to come next because the fun of high school is almost over. Adulthood is approaching and while some have already reached a maturity that has them prepared for life after high school, most others lack that characteristic and still others desperately try to avoid it.

Wrestlers aren't much different in that time is most certainly running out. For Jake and Spencer the mundane ideas of college, grades, ACTs, or job applications are far, far down on the list of priorities. Having missed out on a state title last year, the expectations on them are now very clear and visible where they were almost silent and faint just the season before. This is the season when potential must resolve into performance. The team looks to the two of them for leadership more than they ever have before, but leadership is a tricky thing when you're goal is one of individual success. How do you guide a team of individuals? How do you captain a team when pressure is so squarely placed upon your shoulders and your goal is one of your own achievements? How do you lead a group that will always take the backseat? Some can balance that dilemma, some can't and others make a choice to not even try.

For Spencer, wrestling is not only the sport he loves but it's his social outlet as well. In the off-season he works part time at the restaurant with his mother. So when he isn't wrestling on the mat he will wrestle with school work or the dirty dishes at Gino's Restaurante'. All through middle school and high school he never had much time for friends and activities that didn't involve wrestling. Spending so much time alone, and being one of the best wrestlers in the state kind of sets you apart from the other guys on the team. In order to fit in you might have to tell your coach that you don't want the responsibility of a captain. You just want to be another wrestler but you know that it's not possible. The expectations placed on you makes you different and being a captain would set you apart even more and it's just too much to deal with.

Being a leader isn't suited for everyone, so in the room you try to stay in the shadows and go unnoticed. You don't step out and take the lead. Instead, you lead by example and go about your business going through each drill as if it's your last, working harder than the next guy, training as hard as you ever have, but your responsibility is to yourself, alone. As the captains of the team will yell and bark commands, you remain quiet and are more likely to pick someone up, pat someone's back, or applaud a teammate. You are conscious of the way you are perceived, you have to be. There's enough on your shoulders. Being a captain might be something for Spencer's senior year, but then again, maybe not. Captains should have their life in order. They should have all their ducks in a row. Spencer can't seem to quite get there and it's apparent to him several times each week when the dreams visit him in the middle of the night.

You're about a thousand feet up or maybe it's tens of thousands because you can't see bottom, only fog and mist. It's bottomless, never ending, hopeless and empty. Your eyes clinch in the struggle to hang on. You squeeze your hands and tighten your grip with beads of sweat loosening your grasp. Opening your eyes you see what's at the end of your arm and your eyes meet his. They are always the same, helpless but without emotion and without fear. They have the look and gaze that is both dead and glassy. The sounds that swirl around you are loud but indiscernible. It's all static and noise, both deafening and hypnotic. It's as if you could hear the sound of panic. It's loud, uncontrolled and wild. It's everywhere, and it's nowhere all at the same time.

The grip fails, you see your hands separate and it's only then that you can see the victim's face falling into the abyss. You are again focusing on his dead, empty stare. Today it's your father falling from your grasp, last month the dream ended with you dropping yourself into the nothingness. With each of the scenes, you start to feel yourself falling. It's that sense that there is nothing to catch you and you're completely vulnerable and unprotected. You reach to hold on to something but there is nothing there to save you. You keep falling but there is no landing, you just keep going deeper and deeper and you see your hopes for salvation getting farther and farther away. The alarm rings and you're saved, until the next time.

Life is a bit different for Jake. There was never any question that he would lead this team alongside his father. Unofficially he's always been a captain in the wrestling room. As a father who else would you count on to help get things done? This season, Jake soaks it up and takes the role of captain with an energy that brings new life into his wrestling. Jake seems to thrive and every match has a new intensity and fresh approach. He smiles coming off the mat, not with arrogance but with real joy in what he is doing and understanding of the road he is on. He knows that this is a year that he will never forget. It's once in a lifetime and he will enjoy every moment. Whatever pressure there is on the two boys, it all seems to slide right off the back of the Jackson H.S. captain. Life is very different for the two young leaders of the program. While

Jake walks off the mat with a confident smile Spencer will often walk off with a stoic, if not, sullen look. Where Jake displays the look of conquest, Spencer carries the look of survival with him.

Another practice session: and while Jake's workout is intense, Spencer's workout is more maniacal. Legend has it that Dan Gable used to be so intense and drove so hard during his workouts, that he had to be carried out of the wrestling room. It was said that he wore out all of his opponents during practice and would even take on the heavyweights in the room that outweighed him by over 100 pounds. It seems clear that Spencer sees this season much differently than seasons of the past. His energy is contagious in the room and everyone pushes harder especially anyone that has to go with Spence. This year every drill, every takedown, every shot and every sprawl is in preparation for those last six minutes of the season at the center mat of the state finals.

Sometimes Jake wonders if Spence is having his nightmare right there during the practices. It's almost like that crazy vision haunts him during practices and drives Spencer to new levels of intensity. Most wrestlers are driven by their own desire but Spence may well be driven more by fear and by ghosts. Spence and Tommy Chernich are matched up in one corner of the room and Tommy is muscling Spence but can't keep up with Spence's speed and constant movement. The match is pretty even and the coaches are enjoying the show. Giving up about 45 pounds and a great deal of muscle is too much for Spence and Tommy starts to take over. Chernich understands the weight difference and tries to wrestle with more technique than brawn but weight is weight and he can't magically make himself lighter. The whistle blows and the two comrades break off to opposite sides of the room. Spence is visibly upset and Tommy gives him a hard stare. Did Spence have so little respect for him to think that Tommy would be an easy match? It was almost insulting to have

Spence walk off upset at being beat. Tommy wisely lets it go like a good captain but has it filed away in his memory for the next time they roll in practice.

Tommy, Spence and Jake are the studs of a team that looks to have another strong season. They are missing another senior, Wes Carlson, whose new baby has made it necessary to take on a job and new responsibilities. Carlson has been working all summer and fall and was planning on giving up his senior year. Three weeks into the new season he wants to come back and try to juggle school, wrestling, work and a child. Even with all the support of his parents and his girlfriend's parents, it all might be too much for an 18 year old to handle, even a wrestler. Considering that Wes may not be able to finish the season, Coach Stevens has to determine if he'll even allow Wes to start the season.

Team meetings are to get everyone on the same page and let the team know and understand exactly what is going on and why certain decisions have been made. Sometimes problems are aired and, hopefully, resolved. Today the team gets together and Coach Stevens has to discuss taking Wes Carlson back onto the team. Coach stands as all the wrestlers sit together at the center of the room after practice. Wes stands behind coach and listens attentively with his hands behind his back like an obedient private listening to his general. The wrestlers look up and, like always, hang on every word. Eyes go back and forth between Coach and Carlson while Wes seems visibly uncomfortable, feeling out of place, even guilty as if he just got caught stealing. The whole school knows about Wes' situation, he's the only father in the senior class after all.

There may be times when Carlson cannot be with the team and some special considerations may need to be made for missed practices. Coach makes it clear that this is a special situation and Wes will not be able to attend every Saturday tournament. The team just needs to be able to accept that the rules of the team may need to be bent on occasion. At the same time, Wes will have to earn his position for post season wrestling just like everyone else. Some eyes look over to Mike Fontenetta who is, or was, Carlson's replacement at 135 pounds. Wes coming back onto the team will likely mean splitting time and possibly losing a chance for a post season tournament. Jake fights the urge to turn around and look at Fontenetta's reaction and hits the shoulder of another wrestler who can't resist the same urge, "Turn around and listen!"

The wrestlers are silent as the coach finishes and has Wes step up and speak to the group. Looking over the team, Wes can't tell just how this whole thing is going over. He knows that Fontenetta can't be too happy about it but the rest of the team's reaction is a big question mark. Here he is, asking forgiveness and acceptance for the special treatment he needs in order to be able to be a part of this team. Special treatment is not something that wrestlers ask for. Wrestling is about paying dues and taking the hard road. Wrestling is about commitment, and a team is about working together and counting on one another. He's asking them to allow him to be less committed and less reliable and he's not sure how it will go over. As he begins to speak he can hear his words begin to quiver and feels his throat begins to choke.

"I know some of you might not think this is right and I understand. I just hope you understand that it's my last season and now I have a family…" And before he can say another word that just might trigger his tears to stream down his cheek, Tommy interrupts and stands up like a giant, shadowing over the center of the team.

"Don't worry about it Wes – we're your family too." And the message is clear now that everyone is on the same page. It's understood that Carlson has more commitment and is taking a harder road than anyone else in the room. It's not like he's trying to get away with anything and even though so much of wrestling is faced alone, in this instance they will be facing adversity together.

Practice ends without another word from Coach Stevens. He can't improve on the ending they just had by his captain. Jake and Tommy circle everyone up to the center, "Team on three. 1,2,3...TEAM!" As the crowd of wrestlers break up and Wes gets a few pats on the back and handshakes, he is focused on only one other wrestler. He makes his way to Mike Fontenetta. Carlson grabs Mike's shirt and turns him around. Fontenetta turns and looks at Wes's extended hand. It's the hand of a teammate and of a rival. It's the hand of the wrestler that stands in the way of post season tournaments and the wrestler who just dropped him down one notch on the depth chart. Without hesitation, Mike Fontenetta shakes with one hand and hugs Wes with the other,

"Hey, don't worry about it. We're good." Bitterness is for cowards and any spot that is deserved is a spot that's earned. Both Mike and Wes know that whoever gets the spot at the end of the year, that wrestler will have earned it.

Leaving practice that day Wes feels renewed and better than he's felt in a long time. Driving out of the parking lot he looks over the campus of the school and smiles with a nostalgic feeling taking him over. He just got back a part of his life he thought he'd lost forever. He's been given a gift. He just got back a part of his youth and he knows that even at 18 he doesn't have a lot of youth left. Life has changed a lot in the past year. Prospects for college and life after high school have changed dramatically. "Responsibility" took on an entirely new meaning this past year. Trying to support a child and learning to become a father is a full time commitment all by itself. Adulthood came fast but for the next four months he's able to reclaim a little of his youth. As for now, it's off to the warehouse and working his part time shift.

Driving block after block, passing each home and storefront the reality of his life begins to set in and his smile eventually fades. In that twenty minute drive he will travel from his neighborhood and into his adulthood. Tomorrow morning he may well wake up and find himself middle aged, living in the same town and working at the same warehouse job he is going to now. At the end of this drive his fear is that he'll also find himself at the end of the road. But for his immediate future he has one more wrestling season to look forward to. Crossing the rest of life's bridges will come just a little bit later.

Mike Fontenetta sits in the passenger side of a Ford pick-up and stares into the night not hearing any of his mother's questions about practice or school. Where Carlson gets another shot and another season, Mike feels like something has been taken away. The path to the state tournament just got a lot harder; he now has a huge road block that must be overcome. Carlson has beaten him out of a spot last year and there's no where else to go in the line-up. On another team he might be able to go up a weight class but on a team as solid as Jackson, there's nowhere to go. He has to go through Carlson. Only one wrestler from a team can represent a weight class to compete in post season tournaments and even though he might be one of the top ten or fifteen wrestlers in the entire state at his weight he still might be only number two on his own team. He knows he can't feel sorry for himself. He has to find a way to grip the earth again, now that the rug was just pulled out from underneath him. All he can do is suck it up and win back the spot he thought he already had.

*"There's no elevator to success, you have to take the stairs!"* The sticker on the back of the Jackson team bus is typical of the mindset that is a cornerstone the team. Today they have a tough test against two of the better

teams in the state. Some of the match-ups today will be previews of what will come in the state meet just a couple of months away. Carlson and Fontenetta have taken turns dominating the 135 weight class but the time is coming soon for a wrestle off to determine who will represent the Jackson team in the post season. Jake and Spencer continue their quest for their elusive titles. As the season develops, so do the changes in Spencer Howard. He's reaching that next level that coaches talk about. His intensity is as great as it's ever been. The problem is that sometimes intensity gets in the way of focus and clarity. He's been called for several slams this season and there is a roughness to his wrestling that was never there in the past. Jake generally dismisses it as he appreciates the added aggressiveness and excitement Spencer is bringing to the entire team. Coach Stevens keeps a close eye and wonders where this is all heading in the weeks to come.

With four top teams in the gym, the room is filled with quality wrestlers and eyes scan across the gym all night long. Like lions in the tall grass studying its prey, wrestlers look out for the opposing warriors at their weight class. Scouting each other and weighing their chances of victory they study and tuck information away for later use. The host team, Vernon H.S. is missing from the mats. They are in their practice room warming up privately awaiting the time of their entrance. In the mean time many of the eyes in the room drift to the Jackson wrestlers. Tommy Chernich the senior with as an engaging a smile as he has imposing a figure. Jake and Spencer warm-up on the mat drilling move after move and wrestlers and coaches alike view their technique. It's clear by the precision of each move and counter that Jake and Spencer are at the top of their game and ready for the day. Tommy lies on the mat chewing on a Snickers bar and listens to ACDC on his iPod. If he wasn't busy eating he'd probably fall asleep right there on the mat. Tommy feels himself starting to drift off as he waits for the start of the meet. Then the sound of guitars over the loudspeakers blares through the gym.

"Ironman" by Black Sabbath alerts the crowd and they stand and cheer for their home team. An army of red warm-ups jog through the gym in unison like a well trained company of soldiers. Each soldier looks exactly like the next with their heads hooded and their strides in perfect step. They swarm down upon a mat and begin their warm-up routine. They are well rehearsed, precise and impressive.

Jake looks on with a smile that displays his total indifference to the show. Spence walks behind him and gives a nudge and a sarcastic, "Ooooo scary"

"Yeah, it's a good thing you don't get extra points for the number of tattoos you have, then we'd be in trouble."

Tommy gets up and just says, "What a bunch of clowns! Where's the rest of the circus?"

All that action before a match means nothing. It's what happens during the matches that holds meaning. It's what happens between zero and six minutes that determines success and failure.

In basketball or football the home crowd can be a difference maker. The roar of the crowd during a free throw or before the snap can affect athletes and change the game. The home crowd can pump you up and keeps your adrenaline flowing. Emotions run faster and passions burn hotter with the home crowd. However, on the mat, you barely hear anything around you. There's a din of sound that fills your ears and the crowd is non-existent for each combatant. Many wrestlers will tell you that while they're wrestling, they can't even hear their coaches screaming at the top of their lungs only a few yards away.

The instructions of their coaches were barely necessary on this day for the Jackson wrestlers. Matches are close but few are ever in much doubt. Tommy muscles through his two opponents, each time walking off the mat with a huge smile for the crowd. Jake dismantles his two foes with little trouble. Fontenetta and Carlson split the day and each take on one match and gather in one more victory.

Spencer has a tough second match against Stu Sandover, quick, physical and mean. Last season Spence would have "out-quicked" him, and beat him with technique. That was last season and Spencer is a different wrestler lately. Instead of wrestling from the outside Spencer pounds with Stu head to head and matches each crossface and each club to the head. The match borders between aggressiveness and chaos. The pace is frenetic as the match seems to become more personal. Neither wrestler will back down and the action gets more heated. Coach Stevens isn't sure if he's watching the same wrestler he's coached for the past 10 years.

The final minute approaches and Spencer takes an elbow to the face and blood starts to flow from his nose. Spencer keeps his eyes on Stu as he takes his blood time-out and Coach Stevens attends to his bleeding. Spence stares him down as if his glare will win him the match. Stu ignores Spencer and walks over to his coach. Coach Stevens shouts at Spence to snap him out of it. Looking over to Sandover he sees he's pumped up and so is his coach. Stu will come at Spence hard. "He'll come at you fast, make him chase and go sweep single. You gotta calm down right now, slow down and think! Tie hard and then back off and make him reach. Then you go! Let's go! This takedown wins this thing!"

As they return to the mat the scene plays out just as Coach Stevens described it. It was as if he had scripted the last 45 seconds of the match and each wrestler performed their role to perfection. Spence walks off the mat with a narrow 2 point victory and Coach Stevens feels fortunate to have escaped a match that could have gotten away.

The ride home on the bus has Tommy reading a Spiderman comic book and Carlson taking a long deserved nap from working one of his late shifts last night. Jake and Spence take the back of the bus to make sure the team doesn't get too rowdy and the driver doesn't have a fit.

"Nice match today against Sandover". Spence knows where this is going but doesn't acknowledge the obvious unwanted conversation. "Yeah thanks. It was tough."

Jake presses on. "You know you're not Chernich."

"No, I'm a lot smarter." Just as he makes the remark Tommy laughs out loud to his Spiderman comic.

"No one can beat us Spence. This is our year and then the next year we'll repeat. Don't let the pressure get you. That's just not you out there lately!"

"I'm wrestling better than I ever have"

"No you're not. The way you've been wrestling lately is not any better. You could've won a lot easier today if you didn't wrestle so angry. Sandover can't hold your jock if you wrestle and not take the mat like a punk looking for a fight."

"A punk!? You don't know what you're talking about. I'm fine. I'm undefeated and I'm focused on states. That's it."

By the tone in Spence's voice Jake knows not to push it any farther. They'll probably have this conversation again and maybe it'll be in time for Spence not to screw up the state title.

"Okay, if you say so."

The rest of the bus ride was quiet aside from Chernich's amusement of his Spiderman comic book and Peter Parker. Carlson alternates from snoring to drooling on the bus window. It was mid-season and the tournaments were approaching. Fontenetta looks over at the sleeping Carlson and then stares out the window. In his head, he plays out the match that will determine if he will be able to move on past the regular season. For much of the season he's been splitting time with Wes Carlson but the time is coming when the decision needs to be made about who will be going to the state qualifying tournaments. All season long you work and win with the payoff coming at the end when you can stand up on a podium, by yourself, for yourself. It'll be just a few more weeks before Mike Fontenetta finds out if he will get that opportunity. They will wrestle off soon. If Mike loses he waits until next season. If Wes loses, his career is complete and is only left with the memories of his past seasons.

The sway of the bus and the hum of the tires are just enough to have Spence begin to drift off to sleep. He can hear Carlson snore and Chernich laugh and the squeak of the breaks each time they hit a stop light. He gives up trying to hold on to consciousness and lets his eyes completely shut out the light. At that very moment he sees his hands letting go and hears himself scream as he falls from the cliff. The fog lifts and he sees his own eyes falling into a blur of white. He feels himself falling deeper and deeper sinking down into the unknown. With a jolt he reaches outward to catch himself on the seat in front of him and wakes himself up. There's just a hint of a sweat and if it weren't so dark in the bus it would be easy to see the paleness of his face. It all goes unnoticed as the Jackson team pulls into the school parking lot.

Spence walks off the bus trying to put another episode of his recurring nightmare behind him. The moon gives light to the path that will lead Spence home. The light reflection shines up from the wet pavement and the mist in the air brushes a thin coat of moisture over Spence's face. Looking back he sees the school sign. The bottom portion of the sign is an early reminder that reads, "Parent-Teacher Conferences Feb 21 and 22". Still several weeks away but close enough that the announcement has made the sign's coming events list. The wrestling state finals begin March 4th. The sign is a daily reminder of the end of this season and that time is running out to prepare. He's seen a few of the other wrestlers stare at the sign and each time there is the same pause of recognition. Spence imagines himself walking out onto the center mat for the finals looking at the shadow across from him that is his opponent. The referee motions with his arms for the wrestlers to come to the center. Everything moving in slow motion he looks up to watch the darkness begin to fall away from the wrestler shroud in shadow. Spencer's eyes become fixed to the hidden face that is about to be uncovered.

"Hey! You're not walking home are you?! Get in here!" Tommy's voice is unmistakable and his beat up pick-up rolls up beside Spence. Spencer snaps out of his daydream, smiles, and struggles to open the rusted and dent filled passenger door. Wes Carlson gives the door a strong kick to dislodge the door and the three of them squeal away.

"Hey Spence, daddy here has to get home but do you want to go get some pizza? My sister's working the counter."

Tommy's sister was a year younger but looked like she was 25. No one would ask her out because just about everyone was too afraid of Tommy. Antonito's Pizza always had a good supply of wrestlers coming in and out of the restaurant. The owner loved the business and loved the Chernich's just as much. Most wrestlers would buy a couple of slices and there would always be an extra one on the plate. It was one of the benefits that came with being on the team. Mike Antonito figured he'd always make up for whatever he lost in pizza with all the money the guys spent on pop and playing video games. The place has been around long enough so that he is now entertaining his tenth graduating class of the Jackson team. Mike Antonito is one of those rare fans of the sport who isn't related to a wrestler and has never wrestled himself. But in a way he's adopted the wrestlers as his own.

They drop Wes off and as he walks into his home for a much needed rest. Tommy and Spence watch with sympathy and wonder. It's strange that Wes, the kid they've known since 6th grade, the kid who loves laser tag and xBox, was a father! The boy who sprained his shoulder last year wiping out on his skateboard was now trying to help support and raise his own child and taking on the responsibilities of an adult. Watching him go up the steps to his family's small three bedroom house they don't see him as they once did. They're not sure what to think or how to view him; admiration for what he is doing or sorrow for where he is. One thing is for certain, and that is Wes Carlson is not the same person he was before he became a father. Ever since Janet told him they were pregnant he became more quiet and reserved. Wes stopped being a teenager and had to put his youth behind him. His whole life has taken on the intensity of wrestling a match where every moment is serious and every decision is vital.

When Wes enters the house he phones Janet and checks to see how the baby did today and makes arrangements for tomorrow to see baby Jessica and also have enough time to get to work. Janet's asleep and Wes talks with her mother, who has been the rock through all of this and has been the one who does most of the grunt work in caring for the newborn. Mrs. Powers is a no-nonsense, down to earth Midwesterner who had her first child at 15 and understands what it is to work hard for what she wants. Her daughter having a child so young was not in the plans but things like that never are. Part of life is learning to handle what you're dealt. There is no whining in the Powers household. Mrs. Powers should have been a wrestler.

At Antonito's, Tommy and Spence sit down at one

of the usual booths the wrestlers occupy. It's a small store front pizza place decorated lavishly in Italian stereotype. It's a small joint that has just a handful of seats and does most of its business with deliveries. The florescent lighting bleaches the surroundings and the tiles in front of the video games are dark and worn. There are pictures of Sinatra, DiMaggio, and the Sopranos scattered around the room. The ovens keep the entire place warm and the smell of pizza spills out into the street for the next two blocks. The pizza is sprinkled with spicy chunks of sausage and has small pools of grease to further add to the flavor. The coke is usually a bit flat and syrupy, and the food is served on paper plates in plastic checkered table cloths. As they take their seats, Tommy ignores the fact that Spence can't seem to keep his eyes off his sister. He's kind of used to his friends drooling over Samantha.

"You know coach is worried about you." Tommy starts right off with the same finesse of a blind bull that he has on the wrestling mat.

Spence rolls his eyes and let's out a long sigh as if to say an unspoken, "Not you too Tommy!"

Tommy flashes a huge smile and is completely amused by Spence's reaction. Tommy could care less and knew that it would push a button. "Naw, I just knew I could get a rise from you that's all. The way I figure it is that you're style is becoming more like mine. If it was me wrestling that way coach, wouldn't give me a second thought, but since it's you and it's different, you got everybody wonderin."

Listening makes Spence feel better that someone is on his side and isn't questioning and concerned about his state of mind. Tommy has a friendly way about him although he hides the fact that he wonders about Spence just like their coach and Jake, but at the moment he's far more concerned about getting his pizza order soon. Five slices come to the table all for the Jackson 215 pounder. Tom Chernich weighs a lean and cut 200 lbs. with no excess fat to spare. At this weight he can't get down to last season's 189 lbs, and gives up almost fifteen pounds to his competitors. For Tommy though, it's a blessing because there is no worry about cutting weight and he can eat as much as he wants. It's no wonder he's always smiling. Spence has two slices on his plate and is bewildered as he watches Tommy attack his meal like it was feeding time at the zoo. A single bite will take most of his first slice and Tommy's cheeks puff out as the pizza can barely fit within his mouth.

There's no more talk about wrestling or tournaments or making weight. For the rest of the night at Antonito's they are transformed into two high school kids without a care in the world. They laugh and talk and they are completely engrossed as they talk about nothing. The conversation moves from teachers to girls and then to "YouTube" videos. The topics change rapidly and they don't remain on a single subject for more than a few minutes. None of it matters. Years from now, they will most likely not remember this particular night. It will just blend in with all the other nights that mirror this one. It will add to the memory of their youth, not as a particular remembrance but as part of a larger sum.

# Driving Home

Outside, the un-seasonal warm weather brings some rain and begins to wash away the rest of last week's snow. You can hear the wet tires spin by as cars pass and bring up more mud and dirt onto the sidewalk. As Tommy drives Spence back home, the crisp damp air with the wet pavement along with watching the houses pass as they drive along Spencer's block sends Spence on a trip back in time. Suddenly, he's a small boy driving home from the hospital staring out the window. He remembers watching the houses pass by. Spence recalls just staring out of his window and barely hearing any of his surroundings. The sound of his mother weeping and obviously trying to hold back those tears were faint and muffled. The glass was being sprinkled by a soft rain and every house seemed to look the same as the next as they drove the six miles home that lasted an eternity. His stomach was in a large knot and his heart felt like it was in his throat as he watched each identical home pass by his sight, Spencer kept thinking about going to his home that will be empty and without his father, forever.

They say that time heals all wounds. The pain you experience today will someday subside and eventually disappear. I'm not sure if any of that is entirely true. Especially when you lose a loved one and it happens when you're a child. The pain is still there and it's not really as if you carry it with you. The anguish that you experienced isn't within you, but rather it becomes a part of you. It becomes a part of who you are. It shapes the person you become and time serves only to engrain the pain more profoundly. Pain doesn't fade over time it merely hides and buries itself more and more deeply. The passing years don't allow pain to fade but to fester.

Matthew Howard was a carpenter with a work

ethic he developed while laboring in warehouses and cleaning corner taverns after closing, back when he was just a teenager. By the time he was 25 he had a wife and a child to support. He never had any time for regrets and never thought about the "what could have beens" and the "things he should have done". Hindsight might be twenty- twenty but its blind if you never bother to look back. Matt Howard was one who always looked forward and never wasted a moment looking over his own shoulder. He remembered how one of the first lessons his father taught him was that hard work solves just about anything. It is also one of the first lessons he taught his young son, Spencer. There were many lessons that Spencer learned from his father; throwing a football, starting a campfire, pitching a tent, cleaning a fish, and finishing a double leg takedown. There were many other lessons he would have liked to teach Spencer but time ran out for the two of them. Unlike his father, as hard as he tries, Spencer can't stop looking back and he's not sure if he ever will.

When the doctor walked into the room with the test results Matt knew it was going to be bad news. There was no indication on the doctor's face, it was just a feeling he had that it was going to be bad. The doctor's voice was soft and compassionate but the message was clear and one that did not want to confuse the issue with false hopes. Matt Howard's first thoughts were of his family and of his young wife and son. So many things flashed before him in an instant. He imagined Spencer graduating from high school, he envisioned him getting married, he remembered him as a baby and then he saw him standing alone in the backyard without his dad. His minds eye saw the tears of his wife sitting and mourning with her family. He sensed her helplessness and fear and he felt the emptiness of being unable to remedy her pain. Just as quickly as those images flashed before him, his second thoughts came, and those were the thoughts of fighting, of

58

surviving, of beating this illness. However, fighting cancer isn't like fighting another man or even battling your own demons. It isn't brawn or spirit or even the pure desire to survive that can win this battle. Victory over cancer is a mystery like the disease itself. Falling victim to cancer is falling victim to fate, to destiny, to the unknown. Your enemy is a shadow and your battle is forever.

Matt's battle lasted just over a year and his war left his spirit weakened and body ravaged. There was a point when he realized that his noble battle was no longer for victory but to prolong the war as long as he could. He was fighting for the next month, the next week, the next day. He was fighting for time, and his prize was extra moments with his wife and with his son. Near the end, each night he would close his eyes and hope for another day, and he prayed that saying goodnight to his family wasn't going to be his goodbye as well. Matt Howard left this world not ready to leave it and his wife and son not ready to let him go.

On the last night, the doctor stopped by his hospital bed before going home. He told Matt that he wanted to say goodnight and that he would always remember him. Matt shook his hand and looked him straight in the eyes just like his old man taught him, "Thanks for everything doc". The doctor leaned forward and hugged Matt as both their eyes began to tear. "Okay, I'll see you in the morning all right?" Matt half nodded and slowly closed, and then opened his eyes. They both knew that they would not be seeing each other the next morning.

It was a 400-pound gorilla in the room that no one would talk about. Everyone in the room recognized a fact that no one would mention or acknowledge. There was no more fight left in Matthew David Howard and this evening was one of goodbyes. Spencer didn't know what to think. He knew his dad was dying and that he had cried every night thinking about it. He was also smart

enough to know that he would be crying each night for
some time to come.  Spencer remembers how much sadder
everyone seemed that night.  He walked slowly up to his
father's bedside trying to be brave, and to be gentle, and
then he laid his head on his father's chest.  Matt stroked
his son's hair and they each felt the other crying.  They
held each other tight and then Matt pulled Spencer's arms
up to come closer.  Spencer approached the top of the bed
and gave his father a kiss on the cheek, and received a kiss
of his own.  They stayed face to face and spoke caringly
and softly, there voices slow and trembling.  "I love you
too daddy" with the last words crumbling under the
weight of the young child's grief.

The routine was the same each night for the past
few weeks but this night Spencer and his mom didn't go
home.  There was a special room for families of the
terminally ill. Spencer slept on a couch and the grown-ups
sat, drank coffee and hugged.  The television provided a
faint background sound as they waited.  They talked
about Matt's struggles and his bravery through the past
year.  Each of them had their own last moments with Matt
so that he could say good-bye and his survivors could
have closure.  Spencer was sound asleep, exhausted from
the last few days.  The adults in the room would often
glance over to him with concern and a certain amount of
pity.

A few days before, Matt had his talk with Spencer
as Spencer's mom watched silently at the back of his dark
and quiet hospital room.  Matt had been trying to put
together the words that would prepare his son for what
was to come.  How can a father explain death, life, love,
girls, growing up and tell a son so many important things
in just a few moments?  They talked about God, and
heaven, about trying his best, and being honest, and about
being a man.  They talked about being good for his mother
and remembering that dad is proud of him and would
always be watching. Janice Howard cried and smiled all

at the same time as her husband gave his words of wisdom to young Spence. Spencer didn't quite understand everything his father was telling him but it didn't matter. He did understand that whatever his hero was telling him, it was important. He listened carefully and fought hard not to cry when Matt started to choke up. Spencer couldn't hold on any longer and began to break down. Children understand much more than adults give them credit for and Spencer just gave his father a squeeze and took a deep, but stammered, breath. Then, with a dry mouth he tried to swallow and then bravely forced out some words, "I'll be okay daddy, don't worry."

Janice walked into the family waiting room with her head up as she put on a brave face. It was over. She had just spent her last few moments with her husband and was coming to get Spencer to say a final farewell. She woke up Spencer and he took her by the hand as they walked out into the hallway. Nurses and attendants walked pass unaware of this life changing moment that was facing this mother and child. The noise of the hospital buzzed around them as they made their way to room 845. Young Spencer looked up at his mother as they approached the room but Janice Howard, making every effort to be strong for her son, looked straight ahead and never looked down. Just before entering the room, she picked Spencer up in her arms and told him that daddy had gone to heaven, to not be scared, and that they needed to say goodbye one last time. She carried her child in and they looked at Matt lying in the bed, motionless and peaceful. Spencer heard his own heart pounding, and squeezed his mother's neck and began to cry with an agony he has ever felt before, or since. They sat together in the dark five feet away from his bed. Mother and son clung to each other and shared in their sorrow. Janice rocked her son as she once did when he was just an infant. They cried until there were no longer any tears left to shed and they were both left weakened from their own grief.

They held him once more and then kissed Matthew David Howard one final time.

The drive home was a quiet one as Spencer watched those houses pass by once more on the journey back from the hospital, a journey for which he has become very accustomed. The rain sprinkled on the windows and the puddles splashed the sidewalks as they drove. Spencer watched as they approached their home to begin a new life. It would be a life with only memories of Spencer's father. In his absence, Matt Howard would have his family remember him, but to keep moving forward. That is exactly what Janice and Spencer Howard have been trying to do ever since that drive from the hospital, move forward.

# Wrestle off

Spencer isn't a kid anymore and neither are any of the varsity wrestlers on this Jackson team. Jake, Spence, and Tommy lead a team where every spot is filled with a solid wrestler or even a wrestler who has the potential to place at the state tournament. The toughest group in the practice room has Jake, Spence, Carlson and Fontenetta. They go at it hard and set the bar high for the rest of the practice room. The irony is that there is only room for three of them in the post season. Carlson and Fontenetta will battle tomorrow for the spot at 135 pounds while Jake commands 140 pounds and Spence is the master of 145. With Jake and Spence right in front of them, the only place for Carlson and Fontenetta is 135. Over the last week they've had two other matches in the best of three wrestle off. They are tied with one match remaining to decide whose season will be ending.

The mood in the room is intense. Exams, a season of watching diets, cutting weight, long tournaments each Saturday, and the hours of grueling workouts are taking its toll on some of the wrestlers. Tempers are getting shorter and intensity begins to transform into tension. Aside from Spence's new physical outlook, Fontenetta and Carlson feel the heat of the post season and the possible early end to their own season. Two wrestle while the other two watch the action. After each period, the intensity seems to escalate and the rest of the eyes in the room seem to travel to that end of the mat. Just the other day these four were laughing and joking in the locker room but there is nothing friendly about this session of practice today.

Mike Fontenetta shoots at Carlson but with no room to sprawl, Carlson backs into the wall and loses the takedown. A few seconds later they are back on their feet and Carlson gets pushed back into the wall once more. Now, the unspoken rule in the Jackson wrestling room, especially when practice gets to a certain level of a grind, is that the walls are part of the mat. In other words, the action doesn't stop when you're pressed up against the padded walls, you keep wrestling. Freshmen learn early on, the second they complain about losing a takedown because they ran out of room on the mat, there will undoubtedly be an upper classman nearby to kindly say, "shut up and wrestle". There won't be any yelling or anger, just a matter of fact invitation to, "shut up and wrestle".

Being a senior, Wes Carlson completely understands this, but today, his second time sent into the wall, he responds with a shove to Fontenetta's chest. Mike just gets back into his stance, ready and engages Carlson again on the mat. The fact that Wes is frustrated and mad, has Mike fighting back the urge to smile. Wes shoots for a single and lifts Fontenetta's leg to his hip. Mike counters and kicks his other leg back. During the struggle, they trip over two other wrestlers and Coach Steven's yells out for them to get back to their spot on the mat. Going takedowns again, Wes locks up Mike's arms and upper body and pushes Fontenetta back into the wall, not really trying to get a takedown, but to just push him against the wall. Jake calls for the two of them to break the action and Wes backs off, but Fontenetta doesn't. Mike keeps wrestling and Wes gives him a much harder shove this time. This turns into another shove and it takes a spilt second before the wrestling turns into a brawl on the mat. Each wrestler lands one good punch before team mates break up the scuffle.

With both hearts pumping frantically, they hear their coach shout out to each of them. Coach Stevens sends Fontenetta to the weight room and Carlson to run sprints. There will be no punishments or reprimands, just some time to cool-off. It's tense for both these young men and emotions are bound to spill over from time to time. Practice ends a half hour later and both wrestlers enter the room from opposite doors just as the rest of the team circles up around the coach. They walk right to each other and shake hands without saying a word. They stand side by side, as if nothing had ever happened, and wait for whatever Coach Stevens has to say. Coach Stevens barely looks at the boys showing his confidence that they can handle the situation without any interference. However, he announces to them that their wrestle off will have to wait a couple of days and that they are not to partner with each other until that time. Stevens blames himself for some of the brawl explaining that he shouldn't have had them in the same group so close to their wrestle off and it gives the boys some assurances that their emotional outburst was natural and to be expected. He tells both boys that he wants them to take the next couple of practices to get their heads' right before they wrestle.

After practice, there is nothing said of the scuffle and no one really gives it another thought. The maturity of this team is something that Coach Stevens is very proud of. Many of the wrestlers have been on the mat since they were small. They've seen a lot of scuffles in and outside of the practice room and they've developed a toughness to the point where a few punches thrown isn't going to affect them. That toughness brings about an attitude into the practice room that is to the core of the success of the Jackson team. Practice, pretty much from beginning to end, is serious and hard. That focus is not lost on the freshman or the athletes that are new to the sport. It's an attitude that is contagious and will either infect and harden the meekest in the room, or will eliminate from the room all those who are too soft.

After dinner this evening, Jake drives his brother Jimmy to his wrestling practice as a youth wrestler. Jake picks up Spencer and Tommy and they help out the coaches of the youth club. The boys help coach the kids and try to keep the short attention spans on track and supervise bathroom and water breaks. For their own amusement, the boys also have a running count as to how many times they see a kid stick a finger up his nose. Someone cries about once every other practice and at least once a practice the kids will gang up on one of the high school wrestlers, usually Tommy, and pile on three bodies deep.

The older youth wrestlers however, move with the abilities of high school wrestlers and are the future stars of the Jackson team. They have the same intense look in their eyes that their older counterparts have and it is a rarity to see them smile during a practice. They take over one section of the mat away from the hyperactive balls of energy that spend most of their time with hands in their pants and staring at the ceiling. The younger wrestlers attack with all the aggression of a kitten attacking a ball of yarn. Wrestling is more like playtime at a "Chucky Cheese" than competition between athletes. Jake and his teammates find amusement in helping out. When the coaches stop to give some instruction and the young wrestlers gather along the wall there is one staring out of the window mesmerized by a street light, another lying on his back looking at the ceiling tiles, and yet another who constantly has a finger up his nose. The coach works to demonstrate a move and the kids giggle when he says the word "butt". The room becomes more and more filled with giggles each time he says it. When the young ones begin to practice their new maneuvers, several will make faces and claw their hands just as they did when they went trick or treating not so very long ago. For them, wrestling is more like a fun game. For Tommy, Jake and Spence, it's been too long ago and they have little recollections of when it was like that for them.

The alarm clock rings and Wes Carlson drags himself out of bed. It's just been a few hours since he came home from his night shift and now he needs to get to school in time for his first period American Literature test. The blur from his eyes slowly clear as he stumbles to the shower. His mother has his toast and protein shake ready as usual but this morning Wes opts for some sugar-laden coffee instead. Not much is said this morning, Wes is just too tired. It's been like that ever since taking his part time job. Even when he's not so tired, there just doesn't seem to be as much to talk about. There's always plenty to do but the amount of conversations going on around the kitchen table has dwindled away to almost nothing.

Driving to school, he tries to look over his Literature notes and watch the road at the same time. After about three blocks, he gives up the attempt at last minute studying, confident of at least a "C" on the test. Today is his wrestle off with Fontenetta and his mind focuses on that. Today could be the end of his season. Since he's a senior, it could just be the end.

Mike Fontenetta gets dropped off by his dad and goes right to the cafeteria to wait for first period to begin. He gets a bagel and juice and sits with some of the other wrestlers. Many of them are getting in some more sleep, passed out on their folded arms on the table. Jake is sound asleep while Tommy is on his third bowl of frosted flakes while Spencer looks on in disbelief. It's amazing that Chernich can consume so much, not just because most wrestlers have to watch their weight and nutrition. It's amazing just because human beings in general don't ingest so much on a regular basis. Tommy once ate three gyro sandwiches after a tournament and then stopped off at a McDonald's on the way home later that same night.

Spence nudges Jake and motions for him to look at the Chernich feast. Jake slowly opens his eyes and just smiles in amusement. In the background he sees Carlson approaching the table, "Hey Mikey, here comes your match". Carlson sits with the group and nods to Mike and Fontenetta responds with the same silent nod. Friendly and respectful but certainly not the same type of greeting they would have given each other a few weeks ago.

The day goes by period after period like any other high school.  There is gossip in the bathrooms, testosterone in the hallways, and a mild indifference in the classes.  A small percentage of the teenagers are truly engaged in the class and its lessons while most are doing what they need to in order to survive.  Some are trying to secure a decent grade in the class while others are merely trying to survive the 50 minute period of that day.  Students spend more time staring at the opposite sex in the room than the lecture of the teacher or the board that's being written upon.

Coach Stevens gets a glimpse of the boys walking down the halls and shakes his head for an answer.  There isn't any wiggle room here.  Teams can only enter one wrestler per weight class for the post season and today's wrestle off will solve the dilemma.  Carlson winning would be the easiest solution since Mike Fontenetta is a junior and still has another season to look forward to.  All the wrestlers understand the situation.  In the back of his mind, Mike also understands and realizes that most of his teammates may be hoping he loses today.  He understands why, but it's going to be hard to wrestle in your own practice room and be the bad guy.  Wrestling is really going to be a lonely sport for Mike Fontenetta today.

Practice begins with light drills.  The intensity increases as bodies get warm and loose.  Wes drills with Jake and Mike with Spencer.  They don't look at each other and their eyes never meet.  After drilling Wes and Mike will begin their wrestle-off while the rest of the team goes for a long run through the halls of the school.  Chernich stays back to keep time for the match and will also keep score.  Jake and Spence lead the rest of the team on their run.  They begin slowly and seem to all end up in step with one another, striding together though the halls.  The sound of their footsteps is like a rhythm played on a drum.

Tommy sets up the clock as Wes and Mike "toe the line". They look at each other for the first time all practice, and their handshake takes the form of a quick hand slap and they are ready to go. "Wrestle!"

After spending so much time on the mat together there shouldn't be any surprises. They know each other's moves and strengths. Both wrestlers know that they'll have to pick their spots and Mike is expecting to have a physical but cautious first period. "Takedown, two!" Carlson takes and immediate shot, low and fast, to Fontenetta's ankle and gets the first points of the match. Wes rides tough and wraps his arms around Mike's neck and waist with a "claw" ride. Fontenetta tries to scramble and then Carlson throws in his legs and breaks Mike down flat to the mat.

Jake and Spence lead the team in sprints through one of the far hallways away from the wrestling room. After the tenth sprint, they have a quick team meeting. Jake is the first one to speak and he sounds like a wrestler who is destined to follow in his father's footsteps and lead his own group of young men one day. "In the room right now one of us is getting eliminated from competition and who ever it is, it's going to be one of our best wrestlers. The problem is that if Wes loses, it's the end of his wrestling life. His days of competition will probably be over. It just doesn't seem right."

Spencer steps in, "When you go back into the room I don't want any signs of emotion, or reactions when we find out who won and lost. I want everyone keeping the loser in mind." The two young men lead the way and resume the jog.

Wes and Mike are finishing the second period and Wes is hanging on to a one point lead and also has the choice for the third period. He will take the down position and place Mike in a tough spot because he'll have to ride and turn Carlson or cut him loose and take him down just to tie. His coach would tell him to immediately let him go and try for a takedown right away but there are no coaches during a wrestle off. Coach Stevens officiates the match as assistant coaches look on.

The third period begins with Fontenetta riding tough and trying to break down Carlson. Wes struggles to get away but ends up giving up his wrist and can't escape. Fontenetta tries to tilt Wes and expose his back to the mat and looks up at Coach Stevens only to see him shake his head no and motion his hand up and down signaling that Carlson's back is not exposed and no points are awarded. Time is ticking and both wrestlers steal a glance at the clock. With about a minute left, Carlson is able to get his hand free and begins to free his hips away from Fontenetta. Mike feels that he's losing Wes and lets him go giving up the escape point. He's down by two and looks at the clock to show 55 seconds left to tie the match.

Carlson knows he's close to winning this. All he has to do is wrestle smart, not give up the takedown and stay away. For Fontenetta, time is running out and Wes will be playing defense for the rest of the match. Even if the ref calls Wes for stalling it'll take two stalling calls for one point to be awarded and Mike still loses by one. Fontenetta pushes, and clubs, and tries to get at least the first call for stalling. His wrestling becomes frantic. Carlson is not only a good wrestler but he's a very smart and experienced wrestler as well. He fights Mike with his hands and moves him toward the edge of the mat. Wes wrestles at the edge of the mat and takes a shot that takes the two of them out of bounds. The strategy is a good one because a ref won't call a stalling when you're attacking and shooting but it's a safe attack because you're taking the action out of bounds. That is one reason why college referees will try to insist that the wrestling remain in the center circle.

They go back to the center to start again. Mike knows his time is almost up and he tries a low sweep single and manages to get a good hold of Carlson's left leg at the knee. Now he has to get behind to get his points. Wes pushes Mike's head down to the mat and tries to pull his leg out but only loosens the grip. That's just enough to reach around Fontenetta and grab hold of one of his legs at the thigh. Mike's leg twists awkwardly, and another referee might stop the action but Coach Stevens lets the action go. Now, both wrestlers have each other in almost the same hold with each holding the other's leg. Mike can't keep his grip and Wes continues to work out of the hold. "Two, takedown", for Carlson. Mike pounds the mat with his fist and he knows it's over. Time runs out and the buzzer sounds. The match ends 10-6, Carlson. They stand up and Wes gives his team mate a hug. "Good match" comes out of Fontenetta's mouth almost by reflex.

It's one of those days when things work out for the best. Wes took advantage of the opportunity that was given him, and can extend his wrestling a few more weeks. Fontenetta is a junior and will be right along side Jake and Spencer as one of the three top seniors of the Jackson team…next season. The coaches and Tommy congratulate each wrestler and they all sit together at the side of the mat as the two boys catch their breath. Wes extends his hand again to show his respect, but also as a condolence and an apology for ending Mike's season. The hand is shaken and Mike nods his head with understanding. He just wasn't the better man today. In a few other states, a second wrestler at the same weight class is allowed for post-season tournaments as long as the team total is 14 kids. You can double up in one weight and leave another weight empty. This rule helps to avoid such situations where a quality senior like Wes might have been eliminated from competition. Fortunately, that won't happen in this instance. For Mike Fontenetta, the season isn't quite over; he will continue practices and serve as a training partner for Jake, Spence and Wes. He'll travel, and work-out with the team all the way to the state tournament.  However, for Michael Anthony Fontenetta, his work-outs have now become about next season.  For Wes, it is about a final run and one last attempt to place in the state tournament.

# Junior Regionals

The sun bites down on the morning twilight and Spencer rolls out of bed and looks out onto the mist condensed on his widow. The first thing on his mind is, of course, to check his weight. He stumbles to the bathroom to relieve himself of some water weight. He steps onto his scale gently and softly, as if he could sneak up on it and trick the scale into reading lighter. As he steps he takes a deep exhale in order to eliminate any weight held by the gases that fill his lungs. Spencer is barely hanging on to a "C-" in his Chemistry class. If he were a better Science student, he might realize that he can exhale all he wants but it won't make him any lighter according to the scale. He's right at his weight and takes a spit into the sink trying to get out as much water weight as he can. He even brushes his teeth with care to make sure he doesn't take in any water that may add to his heft. A swish of mouthwash gives more relief to his dry mouth. Looking into the mirror taking some time to awaken to what lies ahead for the day, he is abruptly interrupted, "Booonk – Bonk"

It's Coach and Jake, and Spence is late. He falls over himself as he stumbles to get himself completely dressed and then grabbing his gear on the way to say goodbye to his mother. Spence knocks on the bedroom door and talks through the door "Gotta go mom! He's awake and ready to go. Last night he had no bad dreams and no visions of failure. Today is set to be a day of victory and of triumph.

In a half awakened state, her voice rough and gravelly, Janice Howard calls from her pillow, "I'll see you soon Hun". Tired from a long week she turns for a few more moments of rest before going to the tournament. She'll ride with Sarah Stevens and arrive just in time for the first round of action. She and Sarah haven't seen much of each other this season and it'll be nice to have a cup of coffee and then go watch the matches together. There was a time when they would get together each weekend at tournaments and summer trips but with working full time now, Janice gets little time and has little energy for herself.

Things are a bit different today because today is the Regionals, the qualifying round for the state tournament. Janice takes the day off to make sure she is able to watch every minute of Spencer's matches. She'll get to sit with Sarah and share in watching their sons perform. They'll reminisce about them when they were small and the times when they were the nervous wrestler's moms that cringe with the thought of their child getting hurt. There was a time when Janice couldn't watch Spencer's matches and had to leave the gym and pace in the halls. It's taken some time but she's able to watch without closing her eyes too often. She's certainly not like other parents you'll see in the stands of a wrestling event. Watching your child in combat with another tends to bring out a lot of emotions from a parent. You find the sweetest mother in the stands who bakes cookies on Sundays and volunteers for the PTA during the week, but during her son's match she'll have no difficulty calling the ref something vile and profane. Father's can turn red in rage and shout objections to every call. Fortunately, Janice and Sarah are well past that, or merely above it. These moms seem to get appropriately nervous according to the importance of the match. Experience is easy to recognize, both on the mat, as well as in the stands.

Janice and Sarah stop at a Starbucks to reacquaint before traveling to the tournament. Small talk is the order of the day and Sarah avoids any reference to husbands or work or raising a son as a single parent. The conversation is superficial but comfortable. They chat about the boys, shopping and general gossip. As Sarah talks about the prices at the local grocery store Janice listens but doesn't really hear. They're both anxious to get the tournament started and to see their sons reach the goals that have been the focus for so much of their daily lives. Janice daydreams about the days of Spencer's' youth wrestling, and then even further to when Spence was swinging a plastic bat in the back yard in his diapers.

"Well, I guess we should get moving." Sarah slings her purse over her shoulder and Janice snaps back to real time. She smiles and follows along looking over the strange scene she just experienced, having a feeling of both comfort and anxiety all at the same time. The simple occasion of sitting and having coffee with a friend is a reminder of a time when life was more secure, more comfortable, and safe. Walking out of the coffee shop, it is as though she is letting go of that safe and happy time, and each step brings her closer to insecurity and develops a pit that increasingly grows in her stomach. As she exits, she is walking back into reality and again leaves the place she once had.

Arriving at the tournament, and walking from the parking lot they have to hike through row after row of parked cars that have travelled from countless different counties. The snow crunches as they make their trek across the lot. With all the cars and congestion, they could easily be doing their Christmas shopping at the local mall. The crisp air fogs their breath and clouds of white smoke blow out with each exhale. Wrestling parents and fans donned with jackets that display their allegiance to their high school, trickle in from all directions. It seems as though everyone is wearing their school colors in some way or another. Jackets, hats, and sweatshirts signify where they are from and who they are here for. As usual, Jackson High has a large representation of parents and fans and has several wrestlers competing to take the next step, a trip to the state tournament. Along with Jake, Tommy and Spence, Coach Stevens expects that Wes

Carlson, as well as a few others may succeed in moving on to next week.

Entering the gym, the floor is filled with small groups of wrestlers trying to claim a portion of the mat for their own in order to stretch or to lay and wait for the beginning of the matches. The stands are crowded with parents, and wrestlers who lost last week and did not qualify for today's action. The best teams will have more wrestlers still in the hunt and Jackson is one of those teams with a total of eight wrestlers still alive for competition. Their four best wrestlers are almost a sure thing to move on to the state tournament and the other four have fair chance to get past and go on to the state tournament.

Teammates drill with one another on the mat while others stretch. Some will chat in small groups reacquainting themselves with past opponents and friends, while others will sit stoically and isolate themselves. Most of them will keep one eye open for their competition for the day, sizing them up in preparation for their future battle. A call to clear the mats is announced over the PA system. The national anthem is played and they are ready to wrestle.

On mat 1, Spencer is dismantling a freshman wrestler from across the county in an early mismatch. Jake watches from the stands as he just finished pinning his opponent in the second period of his match. In the background, you hear the shouting of parents and coaches, and the occasional shrill of a referee's whistle. Every so often there is a burst of excitement that will turn the heads of the rest of the crowd who were previously watching another mat. Round after round goes by with a steady stream of anxiety and adrenaline. Each round of action seems to get more intense than the one before it.

Just as it was last season and the many seasons before that, you can witness the end of wrestling careers right before your eyes. Wrestlers fall one by one, as others move on to the next round on route toward a title. Coaches argue and parents cry. Young men and women raise their hands in triumph while others anguish in their defeat. The day trudges along as hopes of some are shattered while the dreams of others survive. The voices of coaches and parents grow hoarse from a long day of yelling encouragement to their wrestlers struggling on the mat. Finally, the last round of competition arrives and the Regional champions will be crowned. Over the loud speaker comes the announcement, "On mat one for the 135 pound championship, Wes Carlson, Jackson and Clarence Golden, Edwardsville".

Wes comes out from under the stands where he's been patiently warming up and awaiting his turn. In the stands, he sees his girlfriend, Janet and their young baby daughter, Jessica, in a baby carrier. Cheers from the Jackson portion of the stands ring through the gym. Coach Stevens and Coach Davis sit in the corner chairs, each wearing the same glare in their eyes. One can imagine them years ago sporting the same intense mask on their faces when they were about to enter into a championship match of their own. Wes slaps their hands on his way to the head table. He checks in and secures his green ankle band to help the referee identify him from his opponent. Never looking at his foe, he turns away and continues to jump from side to side, continuing to stay warm and full of nervous energy. Clarence Golden does the same and never glances at Carlson as he stretches and winds his arms in large circles with his back to the center of the mat. The referee calls them to the center and they immediately turn and step toward each other, face to face in wrestling stances, waiting for the whistle to unleash them.

Clarence Golden is tall and lean with arms that look as though they belong on someone much larger. With only 7% body fat, Golden is a picture of physical perfection and every motion shows ripped muscle. Wes knows he needs a perfect match to stand at the top step of the podium today. He must be aggressive but can't afford costly mistakes. It's a fine line to walk and makes the match a physical chess match. Both wrestlers come out on all cylinders with one attempted shot after another but neither can get enough of an advantage to finish a takedown: attack and defend, attack and defend. They scramble, and twist, and fight each other off for the entire first period.

Golden wins the coin flip in the second period and chooses to start the period in the down position. He could have deferred the choice to Carlson but wants to make sure he gets his escape point while he still has plenty of energy to get out. If Carlson can ride him out, Wes will be in great shape because very few wrestlers have been able to hold him down. When the third period comes around, he'll take the down position and he's sure to escape for a point.

Golden's length works against him and Carlson is able to grab a wrist and keep him on the mat. Wes works on Golden, attempting to turn him for points but, like the first period, they battle back and forth. Golden gets to his feet and works for hand control to escape Carlson's grasp. Just as he feels like he's about to get away, Carlson drops to Golden's legs and brings him back to the mat. The Edwardsville coaches yell for a stalling call but the pleas fall on deaf ears to the official. With 30 seconds left in the period Golden looks as if he's about to get his escape. Carlson has a leg in and works to control an arm but Golden is long and manages to squirm and roll, and the crowd starts to yell "two" for a reversal. The referee points a hand to Carlson signaling that he is still in control. Nearing the edge of the mat they both roll in a flurry of action and Wes seems to end side by side with Golden and the Edwardsville crowd cheers but the referee waves his hands and shakes his head "NO! Out of bounds, no points!" The Edwardsville coaches jump out of their seats and yell for the escape point. The argument goes to the table and the two wrestlers get a needed sip of water from their assistant coaches as the head coaches huddle with the referee explaining the call. The Edwardsville head coach is waving his hands all around and begins to look like a baseball manager who is about to kick dirt on the feet of an umpire. The ref is patient with him and lets him know that he's about to be called for unsportsmanlike conduct. The "discussion" winds down and the score remains 0-0 going into the third.

The whistle blows to start the third period and Carlson explodes with a stand-up only to be picked-up and sent right back down to the mat. Golden catches a wrist and Wes knows he'll have to battle for an escape point. He raises his hips off the ground and supports himself on both hands and feet in a "tripod" and Golden throws in a leg. When Wes comes all the way to his feet the ref calls the situation "potentially dangerous" and stops the action. On the next whistle Wes fights off Golden's attempt to break him down, Wes slides his hip underneath him and comes to his feet. With a grip on Golden's hands, he's able and get away and earn the first point of the match. A takedown can decide the winner and with only a minute left Clarence Golden needs to press the action. Carlson grabs an arm and hangs on. He fakes a shot and makes it look as if he is trying to attack a leg. The senior wrestler knows how to be defensive without getting a stalling call. Time ticks away as Carlson stays away from Golden and keeps the ref off his back. The crowd is calling for a stalling call and the ref raises a fist to warn Wes but it's too late. Time expires and Wes raises his fist and then points to Janet with one hand and covers his heart with the other.

Jake watches the end of the match from the corner of the gym. He focuses on his match and stares expressionless at his teammate getting his hand raised. Spencer is next to him and says something unrecognizable into his ear. Every motion seems to flow without thought or effort. He finds himself on the championship mat waiting the start of his match. His father gives him a slap on his rear and looks him straight in the eye, "Go get 'em!" Jake merely nods his head and all the noise in the gym seems to disappear. The crowd of people turns into background noise like the sound of the ocean when you place a shell to your ear. He can hear the referee, his father, and his own breathing as he toe's the line to begin his match. Jake lunges immediately to the ankle of his opponent and gets a quick takedown. Coach Stevens just looks on with a smile of pride and confidence. Jake is at the top of his game and looks like a state champ as he cradles up his opponent for another three points.

With the sound of the crowd and the headgear tight around their head, it's easy to understand why many can't discern anything in particular when they are in the middle of a match. Jake never had that problem. He's always been able to be focused clearly on his opponent and tune out the crowd but at the same time be able to filter out everything else and clearly hear his coaches yelling from the corner of the mat.

With a five point lead, Jake continues to work for more and lets his opponent up. He scores another takedown by ducking under his opponent's shoulder just as time expires in the first period. Jake starts on bottom for the second period and gets a quick escape and works for another takedown. On the mat, he only sees his opponent, and from the corner of his eye he will occasionally get a glimpse of the referee. The table, the score, the clock, the coaches, and the hundreds of people in the stands all seem out of focus and are a blend of colors. He can hear his feet moving against the mat, the occasional words from the referee, and the grunts of his adversary. The only other sounds that can penetrate are that of his father calling instructions from the coach's chair. His thoughts fly by in sudden flashes, anticipating opportunities to attack. He snaps a head, fakes a shot, pulls an arm, circles, pushes and then backs off. His conscious and subconscious go back and forth controlling every shot and sprawl throughout the match. What he thinks, what he's been conditioned to do, and how he reacts are together, seamless and it all flows through him as he takes full command of the match. The clock ticks to zero with the score 12-5 and Jake is a Regional Champion. Coming off the mat, he gives his father a hug and he is lifted off his feet as Coach Stevens is swept up in pride for his son.

The celebration doesn't last long as Spencer walks onto the mat next. With a win, Jackson H.S. will sweep the 135, 140, and 145 weight classes. After watching Wes and Jake come through, and the excitement of the Jackson fans making noise in the stands and the rest of the team cheering on, there is no way Spence will let this one get away from him. Spence goes out to the mat pumped up and ready to go. His adrenaline gets the best of him and pounds on his rivals head and gives up a penalty point for his roughness. He looks over to the corner and Coach Stevens merely points a finger to his own temple. The message is clear,"Wrestle smart, keep it together." The point seems to snap Spence out of it and he gets back to business at hand. At the end of the day the Jackson team wins all four possible championships with Chernich coming through at 215 pounds. One more Jackson wrestler takes third place and will also move on to the state tournament.

The team gathers for one last word before everyone heads home from this long day of emotion. The coaching staff talks to them about what is in store for them this week. Wes and Vince Vitulli will be going to the big dance for the first time and even though Spence, Tommy and Jake have been there before the coaches give the same speech each season in some form or another. The message is to make the most of it and don't take any of it for granted. For Tommy it's another chance to stand on that top step again and even though the rest of them are not seniors, there are no guarantees, especially in a sport as tough and physical as wrestling. Never take anything for granted. Make the most of the opportunities before you. The time is now. A bad call, an injury, ringworm skin disease, the flu, grade problems, or any of a hundred other things can happen during a season that can prevent you from getting to the last tournament.

"It's something you'll always remember so take it all in and enjoy every moment, but remember to leave it all on the mat because if you don't, it'll be something you'll always have to live with."

# Early Endings

Coach Stevens brings Spencer home this evening and, along with his mother, will have dinner with the Stevens family. The house is intoxicated with the scent of pot roast, catered compliments of Antonito's pizzeria, and a kitchen that warms the entire home reminiscent of a Thanksgiving celebration. The dinner table is beautifully decorated and at first glance, it seems as though the glasses sparkle to illuminate the scene. Soon the room is full of the sounds of forks tinkling against the plates and discussions about next weeks matches, and the season highlights, but will also sway toward topics of school, gas prices, unemployment, town gossip, and what the last episode of Oprah was about. With several workouts before the state meet, the boys can afford the luxury of a good meal tonight and there are no thoughts about cutting weight. At the end of the meal, Jake sits back quietly, and looks around the table. He sees lips moving but everything functions without sound for an instant. A warmth washes over him and he understands that something has been missing the last few months, THIS, the times when he can enjoy the people around him and a release from some of the intensity. Watching his dad just be a dad from time to time and having Spence over to the house and laughing and joking around a dinner table might seem to be simple events, but they've been rarities this season. He sees Spence look around the table in a similar fashion and can't help but to expect that he is feeling the same way.

Early the next Sunday morning Coach Stevens is pouring his coffee into his large travel mug. The morning air still has the remnants of winter and coffee will warm him on his two-hour drive to the state university. Each

summer Coach Stevens serves as one of the coaches for the
university's summer wrestling camp. Wrestlers from all
over will attend the camp to train and learn new technique
from the college wrestlers and coaches from around the
state.  David is making the drive today to meet with some
of the coaches, make plans for this year's camp, and to also
take a look at the new wrestling facility that was recently
built.  With the state tournament just a few days away, it's
not the best timing for this meeting but it's a nice way for
coaches to relax from the intensity of the past few weeks.
It's become a sort of a tradition to meet at this time and for
everyone to discuss the season and how their respective
teams have done in anticipation of the final tournament of
the year.

     The sun is beginning to rise and Coach Stevens
scrapes a thin film of frost from his windshield.  The
approach of spring in the heartland can be the strangest
time of year.  The mornings can hold the chill of winter,
yet by the afternoon the sun begins to provide evidence
that golf, cook-outs and baseball are very much close by.
Driving straight into a sun that is fighting through storm
clouds on the horizon, coach begins to make his way
through the first set of cornfields he will pass through on
the drive.  It'll be miles and miles of the same scenery,
repetitive and quiet for the next two hours and it'll give
David Stevens a nice respite and a chance to think.  The
radio leads his thought process as every other song seems
to illicit some sort of memory.  The oldies station triggers
visions of old concerts, girls in tube tops, bad haircuts, and
ridiculous clothing styles.  Between his reminiscence, he
ponders the state meet this coming weekend.  He knows
that if Jake, Spencer and Tommy wrestle well, they can all
go home with a state title.

     When you're a coach or an athlete in the middle of
your season, the sport, whatever it is, will consume you.
Nothing else is as important and for some, nothing else
seems to exist.  But the rest of the world does go on and

there are other problems and issues that affect all of us, even those of us that wrestle.

Willie Beacham has been driving a truck for the past ten years. As a kid he always wanted to be a police officer but more often than not, ended up on the wrong side of the law. He can remember drinking whiskey with his friends in the back of the playground during lunch time in eighth grade. Once, he was caught smoking his father's cigarettes and his "loving" dad sat Willie in a chair and made him smoke an entire pack, one cigarette after the other. When he finished the last one, his father took the butt and put it out on the back of Willie's hand. It was not surprising for anyone that knew Willie, that he soon developed a full blown drug habit by 16. The first time he tried to kick his habit was in High School. He clearly recalls his aunt putting mattresses on the walls to prevent him from hurting himself. It got so bad that he was eventually strapped into the bed. The home remedy for drug addiction didn't stick and it wasn't long before he was kicked out of the house and on his own.

There was always something good about Willie and the only ones who ever recognized it were his sisters and his very best friends. His drug habit led him to several breaking and entering arrests and he spent most of his adult life in and out of the judicial system. Clean and sober now, he leads a chapter of Narcotics Anonymous and works for a company where he can drive a truck and be home most nights of the week. His young daughter knows nothing of her father's past problems and sees her daddy as a superman, just as all 6 year olds should see their fathers. Having overcome his addiction and now supporting a wife and child, well, he is a bit of a superman.

There are some very strange stories of eerie coincidence throughout time. There is the story about John "Babbacombe" Lee, who was sentenced to hang but the attempts to execute his sentence failed, not once, not even twice, but three times. Unable to execute Mr. Lee, the state later sentenced him to life in prison. He served twenty years of that sentence, was released, and then married his childhood sweetheart. There is also the famous list of coincidences that evolve around Presidents Lincoln and Kennedy. Among them; both men were killed by Southerners in their twenties, both died by gunshot sitting next to their wives, Lincoln happened to have a secretary named Kennedy while Kennedy had a secretary named Lincoln. And then there is the time that Randy Johnson, a pitcher who could throw at speeds up to 100 miles per hour, throws his famous fastball only to have it intercepted by the body of a dove in flight. The incident happened so fast that it looked as if the ball exploded in mid air. Upon instant replay, it's seen that the dove happened to fly at the exact same moment, in the perfect flight path, to be struck directly by a 100 mile per hour fastball. The strange and unexplainable happen each day without any rhyme or reason. Whether it's luck, or the stars, or the mysterious concept of fate, who can say with any certainty?

Today, those mysterious stars seemed to be in perfect alignment, and whoever is the purveyor of all that is fateful was working overtime on this day. It happened, like it usually does, without warning or conscience. Willie was on his regular run and could almost drive this route in his sleep. In front of him are several speeding cars on a highway that seems unusually busy for a Sunday morning. Most cars are travelling at 10-15 miles over the posted limit and the flow is fast but far from an open road. A driver loses track of where he is as he hangs up his cell phone, and changes lanes quickly to get to an exit. A car gets cut off. It swerves, and then a chain of events ensue so quickly that no one is quite certain of its sequence. In the end, there is twisted metal and broken glass to accompany the shattered lives.

Among the six cars involved in the accident, there were only two fatalities; Willie Beacham, and David Stevens. The head blow to Coach Stevens likely knocked him into unconsciousness. He felt no pain and had no final thoughts. He was just…gone. Willie spent his last few moments thinking of his family and the mistakes he made. He was thrown from his truck and laid there in the cool grass and his last vision was that of David Stevens' limp body on the same stretch of grass on which he was lying. Willie looked upon the stranger and wandered what family he too might be leaving behind. Willie could only imagine that he would come to find out in just a moment. He then looked up to a brilliant blue sky and his last thoughts were of his wife and child. Then, a final tear fell across his cheek as his eyes closed very quietly and very slowly.

Wrestlers don't spend much time in the stands of the basketball court. Today they are all there in the empty gymnasium. Half of the lights are on and they already know the reason they are there. Word spreads fast in a small town. Looking across the many young faces, where you would normally see intensity and purpose there are only empty stares and red swollen eyes. These strong toughened young men with the scars and calloused constitutions built from season after season of the world's toughest sport now have the look of young children. Eyes are bloodshot from hours of weeping, their bodies weakened and fatigued by emotions they have never before experienced. As the rest of the wrestlers file in, there is little more than a nod of the head as each young man finds a seat in the stands, close enough to be part of the group but far enough to be comfortably alone. They all bury their heads into their own arms or stare straight ahead avoiding eye contact with anyone else, either ignoring another's tears or trying to hide his own. Most of the parents sit just a few feet away from the group of young men as they all wait in stillness.

The hard soles of the Jackson High School principal break the silence. Following close behind is Coach Davis and the school counselor. Each step echoes throughout the gym and every wrestler's eyes focus on Mr. Jacobson. Tommy, however, sits motionless in the front row with his arms folded, staring trance-like through the hardwood floor, never looking up and trying hard not to think of the past seasons and the man who has been the biggest part of his life for the last six years going back to middle school wrestling. He tries to put himself far away from the reality of the moment and think of absolutely nothing so that maybe he can also feel…absolutely nothing.

Omar Jacobson stands there with his eyes red and his voice weakened and hoarse. There's a slight quiver in his voice that goes undetected by everyone, but himself. He gives the initial account of the accident that ended their coach's life. Police have concluded that the accident was no fault of any driver and that weather conditions and excessive speeds were the main contributors to the incident. The words themselves sound cold and matter of fact but his voice is warm and comforting. Coach Davis steps up and talks about all the lessons that Coach Stevens taught them and that it would be his wish for them to be strong for each other and to get through this together. Tommy continues to stare at the floor as the councilor speaks to the boys about expressing their grief and talking out all the feelings they have. Some of the wrestlers wipe their faces and rub their swollen eyes. The meeting ends with information about the wake and the funeral. When the team departs, it's as though they are saying farewell to each other for a final time. There are tears and tight embraces. They all share each other's shoulder to cry upon and one by one, they file away into the February sunlight. The day is bright and has all the indication of a coming spring. It's odd when the weather outside doesn't suit the tone of the day, when the birds sweetly sing to your sorrow and beams of sunshine bathe over your grief. It is as if God must be telling you something but you can't seem to figure out what.

At home, Jake is helping his mother prepare for his grandparents to arrive. Young James just lies in bed and turns his face to the wall. If he hears anyone come up the stairs, he's sure to be perfectly still so that when they open the door they'll just turn away and let him sleep. During the day he will cling to his mother whenever he gets an opportunity and then, later, he will again cry himself to sleep as he has for the past two nights. Spencer and his mother are there as well. Janice Howard helps out Sarah with dinner while Spencer and Jake clean up the spare room and basement. Not much is said and they keep busy so they don't have to think or talk. Jake answers the ringing phone and before Coach Davis can ask to speak with Jake's mom, Jake tells him that he'll be wrestling tomorrow…and so will Spence.

A few hours later, Spence comes back to the house with Tommy. Under Tommy's arm is the team's electronic scale. They all check their weight and then bundle up for an extended run to sweat off the needed pounds. That is, except for Tommy. He doesn't need to cut any weight and is there because this is the place where he needs to be, he's with his "brothers". They'll go up and down familiar streets and through the park where so much time was spent together as kids. They'll run by the school and around the football field and watch the sun go down behind factory smokestacks. Their shadows will cast long silhouettes as they run together. Each step in time with the next, like they are of the same mind, the same body, and the same heart. As they run back toward Jake's house and go through town, some parents watch as they stride past, watching from their porches and windows as the three young men continue the journey that started so many seasons ago. The mechanics at the gas station stop and watch the young men approach. Watching the boys is like seeing themselves as they were, not too many years ago. The former wrestlers of Coach Stevens put down their tools. They're just a few years older but their hands and faces are warn and weathered, Their hands are covered with grease as one puts out what's left of his cigarette and walks out into the setting sunlight. They stand outside the garage door and their hands begin to slowly and loudly clap for the three boys. Spencer gives them a wave of thanks, Tommy looks straight ahead, and Jake speeds up to the front, as if to run away, and doesn't look back as he wipes the sweat and tears that uncontrollably stream down.

# Junior States

The Jackson High School section is quiet and subdued as all the wrestlers warm up on the mats below. The many different team warm-ups and uniforms lay a wide spectrum of colors around the stadium floor. Parents look for the Jackson wrestlers among the crowd but they cannot be found. The rest of the crowd can't help but to occasionally look to the Jackson section in the stands, partially out of sympathy as well as curiosity. Everyone has heard the news by now that the wrestling community has lost one of their own and they look to witness both the heartache and the courage. Coach Davis sits in the locker room with his five wrestlers. They sit with their heads down as Coach Davis searches to find the words that might soothe their souls and motivate their spirit.

"I'm not going to stand here and tell you to wrestle for Coach. He'd never want me to say something like that, but what happened to coach shows you that there are no guarantees from day to day, so you need to make the most out of THIS day. As hard as it will be, you need to focus on the moment and put your pain behind you for now. You need to be focused for every period, every minute, and every second." He pauses and tries to find the eyes of his wrestlers but each head is down staring at the cold tile floor. "Coach won't be in your corner but you all know that he'll be watching, make him proud."

They come together and all put a hand in the center. Jake puts his hand on the top of the pile with his other hand on Spencer's shoulder.

"Okay guys, look at me. Look at me!" He stops to meet the eyes of each wrestler. Jake's eyes are powerful even though they are red, and dark circles act as shadows to his glare. "No tears today, the season's too long and we've come too far. Let's get it done."

Spence speaks up,"Coach" on three. One, two, three…coach." Other times the break of the huddle would be loud and full of energy but Jake and Spencer's words are too serious to be filled with boisterous energy. The word "Coach" comes out matter of fact and business-like. The tone is almost one of mourning, almost one of defeat. The team walks out together and enters the stadium floor. Janet Powers, holding Wes' daughter over her shoulder, is first to notice the Jackson wrestlers enter the area. She stands and begins to applaud. The rest of the Jackson section follows suit and it takes just a few moments before the rest of the crowd is on their feet saluting the wrestlers who are in the midst of their misery.

Less than an hour later and the stadium floor is filled with action. Eight mats cover the arena. With each match there will be two small sections of fans with a special interest cheering for their wrestler. At other times, the eyes of each spectator will bounce from mat to mat watching whatever action catches their eye. The occasional crowd reaction will refocus attention from match to match and so it will continue for the next few hours until there are only four wrestlers left for each weight that still have a chance to become a state champion.

From time to time, a wrestler or coach or a parent will approach Jake or one of the other Jackson wrestlers and give a condolence. Others awkwardly keep their distance, not knowing what to say or how to act, while still others stay away in order to let the boys have their space and give them time to heal. Jake just nods his head and shakes a hand like he's constantly done for the last few days. Every time he sees someone approach Jake, Spence silently hopes that the well wisher does not come to him as well. It becomes a bit of a game for the boys that whenever they see someone approach a teammate, they wander out of striking distance to avoid being the next victim of their sympathy. How many times can you listen to the words, "I'm sorry", as if they are apologizing for something they have done? Any attempts to block out the events of the past few days are washed away with every person who comes to shake a hand or provide a hug of support. Coach Davis wanted them to all be focused on wrestling today. The odds of that are against them.

Tommy plows through his first two opponents and disposes of them without much fanfare. He looks like a sure bet to win his second state title. Wes Carlson, the senior and the only wrestler with a young daughter in the stands wins his first match but loses his second and must battle through the "losers' bracket" in order to place. Vince Vitulli is a freshman and has been the surprise of the last four weeks. A surprise regional placer he is full of energy and continues the role of dark horse by winning his first match. In the practice room, Vince is always ready to be the clown and the first one to jump on Chernich's back to take on the biggest guy in the room even though Tommy has about a hundred pounds on the freshman. The reality of his Cinderella tale hits when he loses his next two and is eliminated.

Jake and Spencer are expected to go all the way to the finals and should not have any serious competition until they reach the semifinals tomorrow. Throughout the day the Jackson wrestlers go from match to match without the emotion that many of the other wrestlers exhibit. They are far more methodical and reserved. Last season, Tommy took home a state title. Even though Wes has worked so hard this season to get to this point, he has changed a great deal this past year and, as a father and soon to be husband, he has larger concerns and a different perspective than most. Vince is a freshman and, even for a freshman, seems to take everything is stride, but today, winning takes a distant second place to what's been going on in their lives.

Jake's next match is a tough one. The first period goes back and forth with Jake in the lead at the end of two minutes, 6-5. Darren Takashi is coming from nowhere in the wrestling world and is a virtual unknown. It's only his 2nd year as a wrestler but he moves and has the technique of a seasoned grappler. All season long opposing coaches have been scratching their heads and wondering who is this kid? Darren is far from some novice though. He's been competing on mats since he was 5 years old and last year was a junior national finalist in his original sport, Judo. Although the two sports are very different, they share enough similarity that skill in one sport can easily translate into success in the other. Darren is proof of that and has been proving it to unsuspecting wrestlers all season. Jake is fighting to not be his next victim.

The second period starts and Jake can't figure out why he's having such a hard time from this guy. He can feel he's in trouble and looks to the corner of the mat only to see Coach Davis sitting next to the empty chair where his father should be sitting. In the background, behind Coach Davis, Spencer warms up for his match and shouts out something unintelligible to Jake. The second period starts with Darren choosing to wrestle neutral and both wrestlers begin to fight for a takedown. They lock up and suddenly Takashi sneaks a leg in between Jake's and wraps it around Jake's leg like a snake. "Ouchi Gari" is the judo term, the rest of the wrestling crowd simply sees an inside trip. Jake fights to escape and feels his strength begin to wane. He keeps looking to the corner and sees Coach Davis on the edge of his seat yelling for him to get out and score. He lapses in his intensity and Jake finds himself fighting off of his back. He sees the crowd and the lights of the auditorium for a brief moment. Panic helps to trigger enough strength to escape the position and he turns to his stomach but not before he finds himself down by 4 points in the match. He fights for an escape and finds an opening where he can get free enough to get to his feet.

Jake fights to get free from the grasp of his opponent and just as the period ends he gets away. But no, the referee waves his arms in the air and signals that there is no escape and no point is awarded. Coach Davis jumps out of his seat and can't believe the call. The referee just shakes his head and explains," It was after the period ended coach". He is calm and in charge and his demeanor let's the coach know that there will be no argument and the match is moving on to the final period.

Jake looks over to his corner and sees Coach Davis make a few final comments to the patient referee and then looks back at Jake and points to the score board, "You've got two minutes left, let's go!" It's Jake's choice in the third period and he has a decision to make. The lost point is a huge factor because there is a big difference between being down by 3 than by 4. If Jake was down by 3 he could choose down and tie with an escape and a takedown, or he could wrestle on his feet and take him down, release him and then take him down again for a tie. But losing by 4 makes his options tougher to decide. With only two minutes left, Jake needs to get a takedown and turn his man or try to get three takedowns to close the gap. He could take top and try to pin Darren but Jake gets the feeling that trying to turn him isn't the best option. Jake holds both his hands up and signals 'neutral' to the ref.

Jake takes an immediate shot and makes an attempt at a low single leg attack. He gets in but they scramble and Jake fights to get control and his two points. Takashi reaches over Jake's back and grabs a leg of his own and they battle for position. A few times, it seems as though Jake is about to score but Takashi squirms out of danger just enough to avoid giving up the points. Finally there is a break in the back and forth action and the referee raises two fingers in the air and Jake has his takedown. Immediately, he lets Darren go, gives up an escape point, and starts to work for another takedown behind by only three points now. From the other side of the mat, Darren's

coaches are telling him to attack. Winning a takedown
would practically win the match for Takashi. He lunges at
Jakes legs and gets a hold of an ankle but can't seem to
finish. The action takes them near the edge of the mat and
Jake takes a glance at the clock ticking away. Jake drives
into Takashi to force them both out of bounds and the
clock stops with no points awarded.

When the action restarts in the center of the mat
the Jackson stands are clearly concerned and so is Spence
who is sitting next to Coach Davis. He is scheduled to
wrestle on the same mat at the end of this deciding third
period. Time is ticking away and so are Jake's chances for
a state title. The energy and the will just aren't there. The
two battle for control of each other's hands and arms.
Darren makes two half-hearted attempts to get a leg, just
enough to keep the referee from calling stalling on him.
Jake tries to counter but gets nowhere. He glances to the
clock that shows he has less than a minute left to pull this
out. Coach Davis and Spence are out of their seats and
trying to get Jake to get it going. He shoots at Takashi's
legs and gets a hold of a single leg and lifts it in the air.
Darren dives to the mat and reaches underneath him,
almost in a forward roll, and grabs hold of one of Jakes
legs. It's a counter that's even more effective as it is
impressive. The two wrestlers end up in a scramble and it
only serves to take more time off the clock. This time Jake
comes out with the takedown, but time is running out.
The whole Jackson crowd is yelling to let him go but Jake
tries to surprise Takashi with a quick attempt to tilt him to
his back but the referee says that there are no points.
Down by just one point Jake lets his opponent go and
gives up a point, making the lead two points. He'll need a
takedown to push the match to overtime. Jake looks over
to Coach Davis and Spence at the corner of the mat. He
has a look of desperation and fear. He knows it's all about
to end. There's just 20 seconds left and Takashi starts to
run. He keeps his legs back and his hands grab and tie up

Jake. Jake shoots and Takashi sprawls him out and hangs on. The referee immediately holds up his fist and calls "stalling" on Takashi. It's his first warning and no point is awarded, time is running out and Coach Davis takes a few steps forward with his hands on his hips. Spence sits in disbelief as the referee blows his whistle. Time has run out.

The crowd is on its feet and the building is electric. A strange phenomenon is often found at wrestling tournaments and it's never more evident than at the State Finals. The crowds love to see the upset, and will shout and become fully invested in cheering for the best wrestlers to go down in defeat. The crowd is on its feet cheering for the victor as well as the vanquished. Yet just a few short moments ago the fans were on its feet cheering to see Jake fail. However, quite possibly, the cheers are less about the performers but rather the cheers are in appreciation of the performance. A great wrestler losing is the sign of another unsung wrestler achieving success. Another rush of applause flows through the stadium as Darren Takashi has his hand raised. Jake walks to the side and receives a hug from his coach and from his best friend. The tears flow freely and he takes his warm-up jacket to wipe his face. He then turns away and then walks to the center circle of the mat, the crowd stops to watch for what might happen next, and the stadium becomes still.

Jake kneels down and makes the sign of the cross as if he is about to pray. Coach Davis and Spencer stand in shared confusion trying to understand what Jake is doing and then it becomes all too apparent to Spence. In a sudden instant, he recognizes what he is witnessing. Jake is about to say goodbye. He's about to give it up and say goodbye to all that he's worked for, and all that he once shared with his father. This isn't going to be the last match of the season it is going to be his last match, period. He's about to leave it behind and try to remove himself from the strain of his efforts and the agony of his failure. Spence simply calls out, "Don't!" but his words go unheard. Jake looks down and sees the drops of sweat fall to the mat beneath him. He unties his wrestling shoes and leaves them together, neatly at he center of the mat. The crowd stands stunned and slowly begins to applaud. Jake walks toward the edge of the mat and then begins to jog toward the tunnel, almost running away from the recognition the fans are trying to give.

Spencer just stares at the shoes for a moment and it seems that everyone in the building does the same for that short instant. Hundreds of strangers share in the experience and the same suspension of time. The referee begins to reach for the shoes but Spencer runs out to the center and picks them up first. Spencer looks up at the official, "Sorry, he's going to be needing these later." The referee smiles and says that he hopes he will.

"Now wrestling on mat three, at one forty five, from Jackson, Howard: and from Smith, Ulis." Spencer puts the shoes on one of the coach's chairs and pulls off his Jackson H.S. Sweatshirt. He tries to focus on the match he has and block out the emotion of the past 15 minutes. Coach Davis gets in Spence's ear but nothing penetrates. Spence looks up at the Jackson fans in the stands and finds his mother and the concern she wears on her face. She hasn't been to many matches this season and it's been a while since she's felt such anxiety from watching her son. He knows he has to focus but after Jake's match and now seeing his mom in the stands, he suddenly feels his blood rush through him as if he's walking onto the mat for the very first time. His skin feels cold and his hands are clammy. In the background he sees Jake disappear behind the stands and leaving the stadium floor. He makes a mental note that he'll probably find Jake in the locker room after his match.

Stepping into the small circle Spencer can't help but to focus on how cold he feels. He's got a sweat going but it's like he has a cool fall wind blowing on his skin. He slaps his arms and legs in order to warm himself up and awaken his muscles. The ref starts the match and Spence suddenly finds himself getting taken down. Chuck Ulis takes an immediate shot at Spencer's ankle and Spence is scrambling to not give up the quick two points. Spence struggles but everything he does seems a split second too late and he loses the takedown and he fights to get up from the bottom. Ulis gets a leg in and is able to get Spencer's arm and works for a guillotine. There's no way that Spencer would ever get beaten by this painful move on any other day but at this moment he's fighting not to get caught. Ulis pulls Spence's arm as the ref watches closely to make sure the arm doesn't go past a reasonable range of motion. Coach Davis yells at the ref to "Watch the arm!" and the ref just nods his head in acknowledgement. The pain is easily read on Spencer's face as his arm is pulled further and further back. Chuck can't get Spence's arm back enough and takes a chance and jerks it hard. The coach's wince along with Spencer and the referee's whistle stops the action all at the same time. "Potentially dangerous" is the call but it seems that the damage has been done as Spencer struggles to move his arm. He walks to the trainer and stares down Ulis and his coaches. He's not feeling cold any longer. Like a boxer between rounds Ulis' coach takes a squeeze bottle and squirts water into his wrestler's mouth. Spencer's blood begins to boil when he sees the grin on Chuck Ulis' face.

It's just a grin, an acknowledgement that he's started the match in a dominating fashion or just pleasure that he's doing so well against a tough wrestler, but to Spence it is mockery. How dare he laugh at me? Who is this kid that he doesn't take this match seriously? Spencer circles his arm to shake the pain out of his shoulder and takes position on the mat and waits for the whistle to begin. Spence explodes to his feet immediately and moves his hips out and away and works to turn back into Ulis.

They break apart and Spence gets his escape point. Spence takes a quick shot and catches Ulis off guard. It's deep and perfect and Spence takes Ulis high off his feet. Chuck is helpless in the air and looks down at the mat underneath him, preparing for the impact. Spence lifts Ulis' legs to the side and drills his shoulder to the mat. Chuck's shoulder is unfortunately saved because his neck and ear breaks most of the fall and a whistle blows immediately. Slam.

Coaches from both sides of the mat jump to their feet. One coach running to the center of the mat to check out his wrestler and Coach Davis jumps 2 feet off the ground with a "No!" that can be heard throughout the building. "That is NOT a slam!" but somewhere inside he knows that the call is right and he's hoping that something will cause the events of the last 10 seconds to reverse itself. He's hoping for a miracle somewhere along the lines of Superman reversing the rotation of the Earth and making time go backwards. His only hope is that Ulis isn't hurt too bad and has enough pride to continue even though his body aches from being thrown so violently to the ground. As Coach Davis makes his plea to the referee he watches the trainer go to Chuck Ulis in the corner of his eye anticipating the time when he gets up and the match can continue, because if he can't go on, neither can Spencer.

Spencer stands at the edge, knowing that his tournament hopes are in danger of ending right then, and there. His eyes peer to the trainer as she talks to Chuck Ulis and his coach. Then he sees it. The trainer shaking her head left and right and that's all the information he needs to know. Spence throws his arms up in the air and he knows it's over before almost anyone else in the arena does. The trainer tells Ulis and his coach that, "No, he shouldn't continue." The match is over and Spencer loses because of the illegal move. Spence looks up to the stands to see his mother crying and the Jackson fans in various stages of disbelief, many turning their heads as if the scene is just too unbearable to watch.

Tommy sits alone in the waiting area watching in silence and hangs his head. He feels like he's walking in quicksand. Every step, every motion is a chore. He stumbles into the locker room and sits with Jake. "He got DQ'd" is all that is said. Jake stares into space without a response. When Spence walks into the room he tosses Jake his shoes and again, not a sound. There wasn't any tears, there wasn't any lockers getting punched out. They just sat...together, and like wrestlers, together shared in the loneliness.

# New Beginnings

"They've got a good team over there but the uniforms suck!"

"Yeah, the ones with the pirate on the leg, right? Have you met the coach yet?"

"Nope but I'm gonna be working out with the team this summer some. They've got summer duals but I can't wrestle for them officially until winter. And it's not a Pirate; it's a Spartan you retard."

Jake's eyes peer over the lake and drops another line into the water, never looking to Tommy or Spence as they speak. Then he shouts at his brother wading by the shore," Jimmy, stop splashing around your scarrin' all the fish away."

Just then a rare cool breeze hits Jake's face and he lifts his head as if to catch all of it as it passes over the boys. They all turn themselves into the wind to feel some relief from the July heat that grips the lake. Just a few hours after sunrise and the gravel path is getting too hot to walk on. The wildlife churns all around them and the small animals pay little attention to their guests as if the four boys have been part of the natural order of things for hundreds of years. Jimmy wanders downstream taking his stick and poking around at anything that stirs his curiosity. He'll spend much of the day doing this same thing over and over again, drawing in the mud, hunting for crayfish and frogs, or floating on the lake with an old tire inner tube. He loves the yearly camping trips and it never dawns on him that this might be the last one. His mom and Janice Howard will camp from time to time but still, they aren't outdoorsmen. Chances are good the summer tradition may soon be fading out, especially with the Stevens family moving across the state.

With Coach gone, Sarah is going to move closer to

her sisters. She'll have more support there and she's decided it'll be the best thing for the boys now that she's on her own with them. She's always had family around her and going back to her parents and siblings seems like the best thing, to be around family. But to Jake, his family is right here. His family is his mother, his brother, Spencer, Tommy and the rest of the team. His home includes the Jackson wrestling room, locker number 157, the corner table of the cafeteria, and pizza at Antonito's. Traveling 3 hours across the state had nothing to do with anything he considered to be home or family. He's spent most of his life on the mats at Jackson, or so it seemed. How was he going to be able to just up and leave everything he's known and loved? He already lost his father, why does he have to lose everything else too?

"I hear Coach Davis might be getting Wes an assistant's job if Wes can figure out a way to swing the schedule at work." As Tommy talks out loud he looks up at the bright blue sky. The sun was getting higher and they can feel it on their faces as the little shade they had begins to shrink to small patches in the grass. The birds that were so awake earlier in the morning seemed to have tired from the heat as well and their songs have been silenced. Replacing them is the sounds of mosquitoes and beetles and the fishing is about over for the day and, for now, so are the conversations about next season.

They walk back to camp behind Tommy who leads the way wearing his Arizona Wildcat t-shirt. It's the school he'll be attending in the fall and he'll have to leave for football practices soon. Along with football, the two time state champ will also be wrestling for the squad. With the wrestling season well over, he's bulked up quite a bit and almost looks freakishly huge as he walks next to little Jimmy Stevens and chats with him about cartoons and "Tranformers". Behind them, Spence and Jake trade Chuck Norris jokes.

"If Chuck Norris was an animal, he would be a

Chuck Norris!"

"Chuck Norris is so fast that he can race around the world, catch up to himself and pat himself on the back!"

"Chuck Norris can kill two stones with one bird!"

There isn't much to do when you go camping, you fish, hike, swim, canoe, and eat. Everyone brings a book to read but Sarah is the only one that seems to get around to reading a page. This year it isn't just camping and fishing. They'll canoe most of the day tomorrow and get to another camp site so a lot of the days will also be packing and unpacking. Spence figures that keeping busy might be the best thing for everyone. It's what they've all been doing since the season ended, keeping busy. Whether it is to keep their minds off of the past or to prepare for the future, it doesn't really matter. It just makes things easier. At night, Sarah imagines what it was like for the boys when David took them out here and at the same moments she's sure that Jake and James would privately be recalling past trips they had with David.

She looks over at her two boys and sees David in their faces and in how they laugh and move. They're all set to move in a few weeks and the boys haven't complained to her one time, not one. As if they both know that they need to make things easy for their mother and among the lessons learned over the past few months, they've learned that some things are just out of their control.

Jimmy shares a tent with his mother because mom would get scared if he didn't stay with her, at least that's what Jimmy tells the rest of the guys. They all realize the truth is that it's just the other way around. Through one of the tent flaps they can see right up to the sky and Sarah Stevens takes a tight hold of her baby. Young James is nine but he's the youngest and will always be Sarah's "baby". The night is clear and cool with bright specks of light scattered throughout a black backdrop. The stars are so brilliant that you don't even need a lantern to get from tent to tent. Mother and son stare up into the night and Jimmy presses his back up against his mother as if to crawl right inside her warmth and security. "Is he up there?"

"Of course he is honey, and he's watching over us right now."

"I miss him"

Jimmy speaks with the voice that can only remind you that nine years of life is just a blink of an eye. Every bit of precious innocence is revealed within just those three words. Sarah knows that the sadness of those words will never disappear. Young James will miss him today, he'll miss him tomorrow, and he'll miss him years from now. He'll miss him even more when Jimmy has his own sons. Young James will grow up with that "I miss him", and it will be a part of her baby forever, just as it will stay with her, forever.

"I miss him too baby. We'll always miss him."

Coach Davis grew up in the shadows of Wrigley Field in Chicago. As a kid he'd take the train to the park and wait in line on Waveland Avenue for a five dollar Bleacher ticket. He can remember leaving at nine o'clock for a 1 p.m. game so that he and his friends could get choice seats and maybe catch a ball or two during batting practice. The lines would be long even at that early hour since bleacher seats were first come first served. There was no reserved seating in the Bleachers so if you got there early enough you could get a spot right on the wall. Fans would already be lined up on the sidewalk waiting for the ticket booth to open. In that single line you would see representation of every neighborhood, ethnicity, and socio-economic category that made the city of Big Shoulders. Stock brokers having a beer with guys you'd swear must be homeless...all at 9 a.m. Street musicians would be scattered around the stadium with their hat waiting for a donation right next to the brown paper bag that covered their bottle of "Thunderbird".

Kendal Anthony Davis III was brought up going to church every Sunday. Since he was the "third" and he was also the third child, the nickname Trey somehow attached to him. He attended a school with broken down plumbing and paint chipping off the walls. His high school had metal detectors and security guards at each entrance. The rest of his education came mainly from the two block radius of Uptown, once called the "toughest neighborhood" in the country by some television news show. Dad was in and out of the house just like he was often in and out of work. After a while, he was just…out. Mom looked to her faith to help her keep the family together and keep her children safe from harm. To this day, she says a prayer for each of her children. Kendal Anthony III, "Trey", grew up with hard times on hard streets. He remembers his mother buying groceries with food stamps and going to the Salvation Army for a winter coat. To this day he's a regular volunteer at his church and helps organize the Thanksgiving community dinner for those less fortunate. Trey remembers growing up hard. He never got into the habit of smiling very much, but when you got to know him and he did flash the occasional smile at you, and it would be as bright as sunshine.

Becoming the new head coach is uncomfortable for Trey. Before the season started his wife helped put his mind at ease. She told him that there's no one else that Coach would've wanted to take over, and there's no one else that the boys would rather see lead this team. He wasn't replacing Coach Stevens he was honoring him. When you look at the coach's office you can see just that sentiment, because almost nothing has changed. Sarah Stevens wanted Trey to keep for himself, most everything left in her husband's office. Trey decided not to move a thing and just leave the pictures on the wall and the trophies on the file cabinets. It wouldn't feel right any other way.

When Trey came to Jackson High he came to know Coach Stevens and they hit it right off. It was something about the hard work ethic they shared. David Stevens respected Trey's serious business-like attitude and Trey enjoyed Dave's light-hearted way about him. The partnership worked well because of their differences. Trey is a quiet leader while Coach Stevens was vocal and always ready to talk a wrestler up, coaching and motivating at every moment. It was typical to see the two coaches at the edge of the mat with Stevens calling out to his wrestler and seemingly always clapping his hands, while Trey would be standing with his hands on his hip staring intently at the action. Now he will be the one who the wrestlers are looking to and he will be the one in charge of the team's destiny. Not too much will change though, the Jackson team is a solid well-oiled machine and the wrestlers seem to be able to read the subtle expressions Trey Davis provides. Trey might not be the most vocal but he certainly gets his message across.

Spencer steps in as the lone star of the team. It'll be the first time he will be without Coach Stevens and without Jake by his side. It'll also be his last chance to get that state title that has eluded him for the past three years. He remembers that time on the lake after his sophomore year when he talked to Jake about maybe never getting to be state champ. Now, it's the beginning of his senior year and the possibility has hauntingly become very real. He's got to do it this time, plain and simple. What else has all this been for these past 12 years? He's dropped gallons of sweat, ran countless miles, lifted tons of weight, he's sacrificed going to parties, hanging with friends, getting better grades, spending time with his mother, and he has yet to take hold of what he's been reaching for. Not only will he be trying to do it without his coach, for the first time he'll be trying in one final effort, without his best friend in the wrestling room.

The one positive is a big one. Janice Howard has

become the day manager for the restaurant and will be able to be home for Spence for the first time in so many years. She is happier and for the first time since she lost her husband, she feels like she can breathe again. It's funny how such a small thing, something as simple as a change in work hours and a small increase in pay can have such a dramatic affect on a life, on a household, and on a family. Janice smiles more often and so does Spence. It's been a long time since he's been able to come home and have his mother there waiting. It feels good to sit and have dinner with someone instead of having the television remote keep you company. They have their lives in sync again. The two of them live as a family of mother and son instead of roommates under the same roof. Even with all that has gone on in the past few months, Spence seems to be able to deal with things easier, stronger, and happier. After so much crying and hardship, life seems to have finally moved on.

Spence rolls with Wes Carlson in one corner of the practice room and is faster and smoother than ever. There isn't the maniacal intensity of last season where his eyes always had the look a soldier in battle. This season he is merely in another gear. Spence just seems quicker and always seems to be ahead of Wes by one or two moves. That's the way it's been since the start of the season just 3 weeks ago.

"C'mon coach you gotta do better than that. I guess being a daddy makes you old, fast!"

The whistle blows and Spence pops up and Carlson rolls to his back and catches his breathe. The smile on his face shows the humor he finds not just in getting whooped but also in recognizing how out of "wrestling shape" he's become. Carlson rolls over and then forces himself to his feet and calls out to Spence.

"Where do you think you're going? Let's go one more."

Spence turns with a grin and gets ready to face off

with Wes for the next round of live wrestling. Coach Davis blows his whistle and watches his team. He knows that with Jake and Coach gone things will be different this season. Looking at the wrestlers roll and fight and sweat, he knows that with all that will be different this year, there will be even more that will not change at all.

Across the state a similar scene is being played out but a second look reveals something very much different. Coach Anton "Rudi" Rudinoff comes from Chechnya. It is a place where wrestlers are revered and the best of the wrestlers are worshipped. Anton Rudinoff comes from a family of soldiers and wrestlers. Like his father, Rudi has ears that are scarred and puffed. It goes right along with the nose that has a permanent dent at its center from the four times that it's been broken. His ring finger of his left hand is grotesquely twisted from the silver medal match of the World Games. He jammed it on the mat in the first period against an Israeli wrestler. Anton almost passed out from the pain as his coach taped his finger tight enough so that the referee failed to notice the disfigurement and allowed the match to continue. Rudi will show off the finger and tell you the whole story whenever he thinks his team isn't working hard enough or isn't fighting past the discomfort of a little pain. There isn't a wrestler or parent connected with the program that hasn't heard the story…twice. He has thinning hair that forms a bit of a halo at the top of his head. The balding is likely a result of heredity but others will tell you it's from years of wrestling and bridging on the mat.

"No, no, Jake you maaast steap in fraant of heem to exahcute. Is no good dees way."

With the sweat dripping off his nose Jake stares intently at his new coach still finding it difficult to decipher through the thick accent of his new coach. Too tired to speak, Jake nods and grabs his workout partner to do it again.

"Beeater, now you mahst drive heem into the mat!!" You mahst be more aggreeaasive!"

Jake listens to Rudi as he instructs his drills over and over again. Each time he tries to improve upon the previous move to find the combination of moves that will please his coach.

"Leeft eet higher"

"Cahver hees heeps'

"Doo not hesitate!"

"That's eet, goood, goood."

Jake takes a deep breath in relief that he's finally been able to give his coach what he was looking for. Anton Rudinoff places his arm around Jakes shoulders and walks him to one side of the mat as if they were the only people in the room and the 30 or so other wrestlers in the room didn't even exist.

"Leestin Jake. Your technique ees goood baat you must be maach more aggressive. Wrestling is taough sport. You mast be more pheesical."

Jake stares and nods as his understanding is delayed and comes a few seconds after he hears it. Not only does he have to adjust to having another coach after being coached by his father his entire life, he has to learn how to understand him as well. He also has to trust Coach Rudi with his senior year and his final shot at a state title.

The practices here at East Temple H.S. are fairly similar to the Jackson practices. The first different thing you notice is the size of the room. East Temple has a brand new athletic facility and the wrestling room is very similar to any big time university's. There are two large mats end to end with a dividing wall that separates the wrestling area from the cardio and weight equipment utilized only by the wrestlers. There are television monitors at each end of the room that sits below a digital time clock that ticks away each period of work in the practice. At one end of the room, is a crash pad and wrestling dummies where the wrestlers practice their throws. At the opposite end of the room is an open window that leads to a viewing room where visitors and parents can watch the practice. It's state of the art and actually pretty luxurious as wrestling rooms go.

In the coach's office, Rudi has his Silver Medal from the World Games framed and hanging behind his desk. It's a constant reminder of his qualifications to anyone that enters his office and is the first thing that anyone would see walking into the door. On his desk is a picture of his wife right along side another picture. This is a bit larger and sits next to, but a bit in front of, his wife's picture. It is a shot of Rudi, arm in arm with Sergei Belaglosov, arguably the greatest Olympic wrestler in the sport's history. A reporter once pointed out to Rudi that Sergei's picture is in front of his wife's. Rudi's answer to that was that his "wife naver won gold meadal." During that interview Rudi talked about his love and devotion to his sport. His words also gave a clear insight into the mind of Jake's new coach.

"Where I grow up, wrestling ees nahmber one sport of theeee veellahge. We did not have baseball or basketball. We have wrestling and football (soccer). In Russia we have many soldiers in family and war and discipline is way of life. For us, wrestling is much like war. We train and battle. Wrestling is war on mat. It is strateegic, it is pheesicaal. You train and sweat and suffer for victory, to be number one, to be thee beeahst."

Rudi's team has been slowly developing his mindset over the years since he took over the program from Ron Kleinshmidt. Kleinschmidt was a teacher in the school and took over the program after serving as an assistant for several years. He never wrestled and it showed. He viewed the program as one of opportunity for the students at East Temple. He used it as a way to popularize himself with parents and students. Athletic letters were given away like candy. Awards were not recognition of achievement but more of a positive reinforcement for effort. The program didn't attract athletes; it attracted the rest of the student body that weren't good enough to make the cut in the other sports. After a while the word got out about the program and marginal athletes that wanted a varsity letter on their college application would go out for the wrestling team. Behind the scenes, the other coaches and athletes laughed at the wrestling program and there were very few quality athletes signing up to join the team. It's easy to survive as a bad wrestling coach because most athletic directors simply don't know enough about the sport or even care about the program at all.

Parents loved Kleinschmidt because he gave their sons a place to belong and the delusion that they were worthy of an athletic award and the ability to walk through the school halls with a letterman's sweater. It was a program of perceived achievements and fabricated successes. But all of that was before Anton Rudinoff took over the program.

Today, the other jocks in the school walk lightly around the wrestlers. The programs around the state are learning about the East Temple program. Rudi has his team rough and ready for all comers. If unnecessary roughness was a category in the record books, the East Temple team would lead all programs across the state. There are some coaches that fear for their wrestlers each time they have to step foot on the mat with an East Temple opponent. The wrestlers and the parents alike, take pride in the style they have adopted. They follow the word of their world renowned coach like Moses leading them across the Red Sea. Now Jake is the next to become a part of his flock.

# Setting the Stage

Leo Hall is the captain of the East Temple team. Last year he was suspended for fighting and was almost put in jail for breaking a students arm. His father was in the state penitentiary for the sale of narcotics and after this year he plans on having no plans for his future. He had an engaging smile that was in direct contrast to his hair trigger temper. The wrestling team kept him out of trouble since any misstep would mean suspension from the team, and was a vehicle to let out all his aggression. Rudi loved him right away and knew he was perfect to have as his captain. He embodied all that Rudi was trying to build and was the perfect person to turn the program around from the softness of the Kleinschmidt era and into the program of toughness that Rudi demanded. In just 4 seasons Rudi has taken the East Temple program from obscurity to the brink of being a contender and Jake will be the next piece to the puzzle.

"Leeaht's go gentlemen; there are no cowards on theees team. We go 'till we can not go no more, and then we go a leettle further."

Rudi's words ring through the room as the wrestlers push through yet another drill. Leo Hall goes over to the corner and gets right into the face of one of the nameless sophomores. He's a heavier wrestler who joined the team because he was cut from football. He didn't get the memo that the Kleinschmidt wrestling team no longer resided at East Temple.

"What the hell are you doing on this team? You haven't lost a pound since you've joined. You aren't working!!"

The answer was clear. The young wrestler didn't work hard enough, didn't sacrifice, he didn't belong. Two weeks later he will have realized that fact and will spend his time knowing that wrestling was not the right sport for him to try.

Coach Rudi ignores his captain's rant because Leo's words are the exact words he'd like to say. Leo is able to get Rudi's messages across without Rudi having to say them. Jake watches as if he's from the outside looking in. Life in this wrestling room is very different from his experience. He lives on the edge of a fence every practice. Sometimes he tilts to one side and thinks that he can't wrestle for this team and most other times he thrives on the intensity and aggressiveness that fills the room. Wrestlers hide their aches and pains and most have a constant mask of bravado. "Crossfaces", where a wrestler takes his forearm and rakes it across his opponents face are thrown from a wind-up and wrestlers are returned to the mat with severe authority. There is viciousness in the wrestling in the East Temple room. The athletes compete more with brutality than technique, more with anger than competitiveness. Jake recognized that there were definite differences in this wrestling room, but he is feeling more and more accustomed to it.

Driving your partner into the wall and then drilling him into the mat can give you a strange satisfaction and definitely gives you a real sense of power. The wrestlers on the Spartan team feed off of that feeling and you can see it, not only in the way they wrestle but in the way they carry themselves, the way they talk, the way they walk, and the way they seem to look right through you as if they were letting you know of your own insignificance.

Today, like most days in his career, Jake gets the best of his workout partner and he has a concentration that wasn't there in season's past. In the back of his mind he replays his match from a few days earlier, his first match as an East Temple Spartan. As he watches from the side waiting for his turn on the mat he can see himself driving his head into the bridge of his opponent's nose and then later slamming him into the mat giving up a penalty point. He remembers the pump he felt as his hand was raised and the shear rush of power that came with the victory. He was invincible and he felt every morsel of that invincibility. Leo ran up and slapped his back as if to say, "Welcome, you're now a Spartan."

One of the coaches walks into the room with a newspaper in hand, clearly turned to the sports section. It was Tuesday and the local paper devoted much of its sports space to high school reporting on this day. Taking a split second glance, Jake recognizes the picture on the page immediately. It's a wrestler, and he's wearing a Jackson singlet. If a Jackson wrestler was going to have a big color picture in the paper, the chances were good that the wrestler was going to be Spence. Jake walks right over to the coach and takes the paper from his hand. Sure enough, there was Spence in full color, disposing of another wrestler. The byline under the picture catches his eye. He stares at it and reads it three times before putting the paper down. Without saying a word he goes back to the mat and restarts his workout.

The assistant coach with the paper knew exactly what Jake was looking at and studied Jakes reaction as he returned to practicing. The young coach said nothing because there was nothing to say. Jake was hoping that Spence would be going up a weight-class to 152 lbs. but as it happened the paper lists him as wrestling at 145 in a tournament last weekend. So now it seems like for the first time in their high school careers they will be on different teams and at the same weight class. This is the last chance for a state title for each of them but now only one will be able to achieve it. Jake was too big to make last season's 140 lbs. and Spence would be undersized at 152. There was no avoiding it. The course was set and it was set for a collision.

It was a week later when new rankings came out and showed Spence ranked first and Jake second at 145.

There really was no doubt about the top two wrestlers at the weight. Jake and Spence were the best wrestlers to have never won a state title and the rest of the state was simply a tier below. Some top wrestlers moving up a weight class or two, a couple of others transferring schools to a different division led to a weight class where Jake and Spence were the class of the weight. It was Spencer, Jake and then the rest of the field vying for third place. The simple fact was that Spence might be able to win it at 152 but he was definitely stronger at 145 and so was the Jackson team. There simply was no avoiding it. They were both trapped in the situation and only one will be able to achieve the goal that has eluded them for the past three seasons.

The phone rang Tuesday evening as soon as Jake came home from practice. Spencer had an idea who would be on the other line when he picked up the receiver. He wasn't surprised to hear Jake's voice on the other end. "I hope you're getting used to the idea of a silver medal in March."

"Silver makes my skin turn green. I think I'll pass on that."

"Why are you going 145? Not tough enough for 52?"

"Ha! Hey Jake, there's talk about a girls league in a few years, maybe you could have done good in that."

"No thanks, now that I'm in East Temple I'm getting used to tough competition. Maybe the Jackson team can win a second or third place if they make a girls tournament!"

Then an awkward pause interrupts the back and forth exchange. They both struggle for the next words and Jake finally breaks the moment.

"So really, how hard is it for you to make 45?

"I won't be able to do it for every tournament all year but coach wanted to see if it'd be a problem for me to make the weight. We're definitely stronger as a team with me at 145. When I wrestle up we end up with hole at 135 and we're already kindof weak in a few other spots. When post season comes around I should be able to stay down to the lower weight. You're not too scared are you?"

"No, I figure you're tough enough to take the beating I'm gonna give you."

"We'll just have to see how it all ends up Jake. How's the new team doing? What's Rudinoff like?

"Rudi's pretty intense. He's like an Eastern Block Tommy Chernich. It's kindof a different style over here. I already have a lot of bruises. How's Coach Davis?"

"He's good, so is Carlson. We already had a practice with Six's."

Six's is a test of endurance and heart. Wrestlers went three periods with the periods lasting six minutes each. It is the equivalent of three full matches with no breaks in between. Then after the eighteen minutes of wrestling, the wrestlers drag themselves into the gym and do six sprints, six trips up and down the stands, and finally jog six long laps through the halls. Coach always made sure there were a few garbage cans around for those who needed to puke out their lunch in the middle of the "Six's". It's a regimen that the wrestlers hate to go through but take pride in after the fact. It's just another badge of honor they can attach to their inner vest of pride that cloaks the heart of a wrestler.

The two friends talk for another half hour or so and banter about wrestling and school and the occasional reference to the camping trip. All the while, in the back of their minds, each of them think about the prospects of losing to the other and taking a second place and finishing one step short of the state championship podium.

"Okay, I gotta go. Good luck on the rest of the season."

"Yeah, I guess I'll see you in the finals."

"That's up to you…I know I'll be there!"

# Blathowick Tournament

The Blathowick tournament is relatively new, but has become one of the toughest in the state. It has steadily grown for the past 5 years and many schools are waiting their chance to be included into the field. In the past two seasons the tournament has featured several state placers at each weight class and is becoming a measuring stick to see who the contenders are and who the pretenders are.

Marc Blathowick was a wrestler at Kennedy High. He was new to the sport and a solid wrestler for the brief amount of time he had on the mat. He was looking forward to a solid senior year when a drunk driver struck his motorcycle and knocked him 75 feet across the pavement. He had no warning, no helmet, and no chance. His wake was filled with students and teachers. On his coffin was his junior year picture. His familiar smile added to the disbelief that he was actually gone. Wrestlers sat together at the side of the room while a group of girls cried in each other's arms in the back of the hall. At an age when kids feel immortal, the reality of this very moment will be carried with them well into their old age. For some, they will carry the images of that day as vividly as any joyous occasion they will recall. It's a moment of loss; loss of life, loss of youth, and a loss of innocence.

Today, the gym is filled with another gathering of all-star caliber wrestlers. Jackson High is about two and a half hours away from Kennedy and is not on the list of teams. Coach Davis contemplates making the long trip one year but for now they will read about the competition in the papers, and there should be plenty to read about. Jake is gearing up in the corner of the gym, hopping up and down in a wrestler's "shuffle" that is so familiar to those in the sport. He hops up and down from one side to

119

the other.  After a while he finally breaks a small sweat and feels some of the kinks and soreness from the practice room fade away.  Even with all the talent in the gym, he knows that there shouldn't be anyone to challenge him today.  Rudi sits with some parents and talks about the competition on the mat and how the Spartan team should match up today.  Many of the parents cling to his every word as both his ego and reputation continue to grow.

Jake watches from the gym floor.  With all the respect he has for his new coach he knows that there is more to being a coach than medals on display and a resume of achievements.  It's his first big tournament since leaving Jackson.  It's his first big tournament without his father and he sees Rudi sitting in the stands glowing from all the attention he not only receives but seems to demand.  His resentment toward Rudi is confusing.  He's just a coach and more importantly, he was HIS coach now.  Jake thinks to himself he shouldn't be having these feelings and his bitterness turns to anger as he bobs up and down awaiting his name to be called for his match.

He clinches his fist in that anger, an anger toward Rudi for simply not being his father, for the truck driver that hit his father's car, for his father for dying, for all the parents who love Rudi so much, for Spence who is wrestling at 145 this year, and for himself for not being able to sort all of this out for himself.  The anger becomes just this soup of chaos that Jake stirs and heartily devours.

"At 145 on mat one, Stevens, East Temple and Johnson, Lakeview."

Rudi is a relatively calm coach in the corner of the mat.  Like many coaches he believes that shouting out instructions is a waste of time.

"Eef your wrestler doesn't know what to do, hee maast not be ready to wrestle."

He saves his instruction for strategy and to send messages to the referees.  His style works well for the accomplished and seasoned wrestlers, like Jake.  Jake really doesn't need too much help from the side. The occasional reminder of the clock and the number of stalling warnings is about all he needs. Jake is savvy and keeps track of the score in his head and will take the occasional look at the clock to check the time and score during the match. His first two matches go smoothly except for the badgering he gets from Rudi after his wins.

"Jake you need to peek ahp the eentensity now. You cannot win state title, wrestling so-so. You mahst be aggreeassive and punish your opponent, put heem away. Do you understand?"

Jake just looks straight ahead as Rudi is talking into his ear. His next win puts him into the finals but he wants to make a statement. A statement that says that he's the class of this tournament and there is no one else but him that should be considered to have the top spot at 145, not even Spencer Howard.

Jake leads the match 5-1 in the second period and Rudi stands up and tells him to pick it up. "Eentensity!" is all he says and Jake just nods his head. Jake lets his opponent go and they go on their feet making the score 5-2, but the numbers are of no consequence. There is never any doubt as to who would come out on top of this one. Jake goes in on a slick low single leg attack that is so fast that some people in the stands miss it with one quick glance to a different mat. The Lakeview wrestler quickly stands up and is picked up and crashed back to the mat. The Lakeview coach yells for a slam but the referee ignores his pleas. Jake throws a leg in and works a guillotine. Jake takes his opponent's arm and pulls it back in a way that it makes some in the stands empathize and contort their faces in pain for the boy.

"Hey! C'mon watch the arm!!"

Finally, the referee blows his whistle and stops the action for a potentially dangerous hold. The young Lakeview wrestler tries to hide his pain as he moves his shoulder around and around and rubs it back into shape.

In Jake's corner, Rudi claps his hands and tells Jake to keep it up. As the match starts again, Jake throws in a leg again and pulls the same arm again into the same painful contortion. The Lakeview wrestler just wasn't good enough to beat Jake but he was good enough and tough enough to not give up this move to Jake and go to his back. All this creates is a weird scenario. If he was better he'd be more competitive with Jake and there might be less punishment. If he was worse, Jake would have pinned him by now and again, there would be less punishment. As it is, Jake tears at his arm and at first glance his shoulder looks like the arm is fractions away from coming out of its socket. Another whistle and the Lakeview coach yells at the ref to take control of the match. Rudi can't stand it any longer.

"Deed your boys come to wrestle or to whine? Thees eees a touaagh sport coach."

"Shut your mouth coach, I'll take care of my boys!"

The match starts once more and Jake is working for another takedown. He slides under the Lakeview wrestler's arm and grabs him around his waist. In one big step to the side he launches the Lakeview wrestler in the air and they both land with a loud thud. The whistle immediately blows and the referee calls an illegal slam.

Steve Anderson from Lakeview lies on his back for a few moments and his coach tells him to stay down until he gets checked out by the athletic trainer. Steve is tall and thin and looks more like a high jumper than a wrestler. He holds a 4.5 GPA and is an eagle scout. He wasn't going to beat Jake and he sure wasn't going to lie down and win by a DQ. He was going to finish this match.

Once again the match begins and Jake tears at Anderson's arm once more. Jake is ruthless and unrelenting. The match comes to a merciful end as Jake finally turns Anderson and wins by a fall. Jake shakes hands with Anderson and the Lakeview coach as if nothing was out of the ordinary and the match was like any other. But all those involved knew that it wasn't. Jake gave Anderson a beating. The match could have been won without the brutality that was so uncharacteristic for Jake. But this was a new team, and a new Jake.

The stands took notice of how dominant and physical Jake was. It was impressive to see such forceful control of another wrestler. Rudi places his arm around Jake and lets him know how pleased he is with the performance.

"That ees the kind of eentensity and toughness I've been looking for Jake"

They walk off with Rudi yapping into Jake's ear and slapping him on the back in encouragement. Jake succeeded in his goal. The statement was made. There was no one in the stands that had much doubt about who will be the state champ at 145 this year. In their minds, they just saw him.

It felt good to be the star, the only star. No one else shining as bright and having the entire spotlight for himself. Sure there were other tough wrestlers on the East Temple team but in reality none, of them had much chance of going all the way this season. They were aggressive and some bordered on criminally dangerous, but even Leo Hall lacked a certain amount of skill and technique to take him to the very top step. It was all about Jake on this team and it felt good.

On the other side of the state it was business as usual for the grapplers in Jackson. Wes Carlson has put on a few pounds and is usually going with Spence. With Jake gone, Coach Davis is always on the lookout for opportunities to have someone of quality to come in and roll with Spence. Today it's Nick Ortega. Nick was a stud for Jackson several years back. He placed at the state tournament 3 times but never won it all. His senior season was plagued with injuries and had to battle the flu during the state tournament. It's not something he ponders. It's past him. He went on to wrestle for a Division II team and was an All-American both his junior and senior years. Now days he spends his time trying to keep his construction business afloat, but as a favor to the program and out of an obligation to Coach Stevens, he comes in once or twice a week to roll with Spence.

Coach Davis watches from the other side of the mat as Nick and Spence go at it. Between takedowns and scrambles there are smiles on their faces as they both enjoy the competition and feeling of technique against technique. The competitiveness is alive with energy and it fills the room. The whole atmosphere in the wrestling room is remarkably light these days. It seems that whatever mourning that needed to go on for Coach Stevens, it has been completed and the boys have been able to move past their loss, or at least they make it seem as such.

Maybe it's because Spence is in good moods lately since he sees his mother daily and goes home to a family. It's just the two of them but it's a family nonetheless. It's as if the rest of the team feeds off of Spencer's positive emotion. Maybe it's because they realize there are more important things than this sport they kill themselves over. They learned a life lesson with Coach's death. There just might be a new perspective in the room and even though wrestling is the most important thing in their lives at the moment, they understand it's not the most important thing in the world. Maybe it's because they're back to doing the thing that's most normal to them, the thing where they feel the most comfortable. They're back on the mat and working hard and they can start to put the sorrow and the loss behind them.

# Adjustments

*"Things aren't the way they were before.*
*You wouldn't even recognize me anymore.*
*Not that you knew me back then*
*But it all comes back to me. In the end*
*I tried so hard and got so far*
*but in the end it doesn't even matter.*
*I had to fall to lose it all*
*but in the end it doesn't even matter..." Linkn Park*

The music blares through the weight room and Jake's eyes stare straight through everyone he sees, moving from one lift to the next with a clear urgency, as if he needed to get his workout done hours ago. Between sets, he paces quickly around the room and ignores those who are less serious about their workout. He walks past those who stand and small talk between lifting. For Jake every minute is as intense as each minute of a match. The lyrics of the Linkn Park song ring in his head as he pumps out his next set of squats. While others may lift with intensity, Jake lifts with emotion, with passion, and sometimes with a fury. With so much emotion and effort, there are actually times when Jake feels like he may break down and cry. He just shakes his head and wipes his eyes as if they're irritated. He has no idea why this happens or if it happens to anyone else, but he doesn't care and can't stop to think about it anyway.

Jake walks to the squat rack and throws on two 25 lb. plates making the total 275 lbs that his 150 or so pounds will carry. The squat is a tough movement and is sometimes called the king of all lifting exercises. Jake takes a deep breath and fills his lungs before he begins his squat. The blood immediately begins to rush to his face and he can feel the pressure of the air in his lungs begin to build. Jake drives up with his eyes straining to look to the ceiling in an attempt to keep his head up and his body moving up through the squat. The fifth rep is tough. His body starts to shake in the middle of the motion and he finishes with a small yell to help him complete the lift. Jake takes some small steps to rack the bar and immediately goes to the water fountain without so much as looking at another face in the room because no one exists for him right now and no one else matters.

It's after his regular practice and now it's after his lifting routine. Jake is sufficiently spent. There's a kind of relief in expending all your energy and losing yourself in your efforts. Some people might see this exhaustion as a burden while others, like Jake, achieve a sense of enlightenment, or satisfaction. There seems to be a cleansing of sorts in the process. You rid yourself of all energies and emotions. All the negatives and the frustrations leave the body and you're left with a blank slate, an empty canvas. There is no joy but there is no pain, there is no happiness but also, no sorrows. You feel better because the bad stuff is gone even though everything else seems to be gone along with it. Sometimes it just feels better to be empty.

Jake sits outside the gym waiting in the hall for some of the other guys. The halls are vast and wide at East Temple and coach Rudi almost doesn't even notice his new star sitting at the end of the hall.

"Hey Jake, whaat's thee matter?"

"Not a thing coach, just waiting for Leo to get out."

"Okayeee, make sure to get enough sleep. Beeg day tomorrow."

Every day was a big day for Rudi. His intensity was constant and his focus is always on the sport. The "beeg day" was just another meet with a few teams that East Temple will have no trouble disposing of. Rudi liked to have his team always on edge and ready for a battle no matter who the opponent is.

"Yeah, I will coach."

Calling someone else "coach" was still strange for Jake but it was something he's been able to adjust to. He's been to a lot of camps and summer teams so he's had many other coaches give him instruction but whenever he says the word there is something in the word that will always be meant for his father.

The East Temple is a large modern school with the benefit of a planned architecture that allows for several gyms laid out to the exact specifics for its sports programs. East Temple has a gym area that is reserved primarily for wrestling and volleyball. The size of the gym perfectly fits two mats with enough room for four teams to sit comfortably. There's a small set of stands on both sides that make the surroundings both intimate and more than adequate. Like most wrestling meets the East Temple stands are only partially filled with a few parents. Even though there are only a few regulars, what the group lacks in numbers, they make up for in volume. Both the dads and moms aren't afraid to let their voices be heard. While, some of the wrestlers cringe when they hear their mother yell and scream, most take it all in stride and they all give a chuckle when they hear Mrs. Hall yell for the referee to make the right call. Although she herself might not yet know all the rules, if things aren't going Leo's way it must be the fault of the referee, it just must. After the match, she will always smile and laugh at herself but in the heat of the moment she is all business and there is no one who is as serious as she.

The crowds have been getting larger in the East Temple wrestling gym these past few years. The type of wrestling that Rudi has brought to the school is aggressive, it's exciting, and it wins. More and more students are coming around to the wrestling matches to see some of the school's tough guys mix it up. The athletes joining the team are no longer the outcasts and misfits.  The better athletes are making their way toward the wrestling room and that also brings in the interest of others into the gym to watch the match; friends, girlfriends, and even some teachers.  Today the stands are still mostly bare but it's far better than in seasons past.

As the matches get underway Jake studies Rudi closely, almost like a detective eyeing a suspect.  He just watches what Rudi will do next, not quite knowing what to expect.  The night unfolds with several tough loses.  Unfortunately, all of the close losses are for the Spartans and the contest is much closer than it should be going into the last two matches.  At 215 lbs. East Temple's Josh Baker is feeling the effects of a flu bug that's sneaking up on him.  He has no idea why he is feeling slow and weak; he only knows that his coach is on the edge of the mat letting him know how unhappy he is about the performance.  The team score has the Spartans up by just 4 points and a win would guarantee victory but Josh just can't get anything going.  With just a minute to go in the third and final period Josh makes a half hearted attempt at a double leg but is countered and suddenly finds himself on his back.  He tries to turn and roll out of the predicament but the next thing he hears is the sound of the referee slapping the mat.

Rudi jumps in the air beside himself and almost falls backward upon landing.  The faces of the East Temple team drop their collective jaws.  They are now losing by 2 team points and could lose the entire match.  It will be up to their 285 pounder, "Big Moe", to win his match and save the team from an unlikely and embarrassing loss.  In the corner of the gym "Big Moe" is warming up and watches Josh get stuck.  He knows how important his match is even before Rudi comes to his side and points out the scoreboard.  After fourteen matches and over an hour of wrestling the outcome of the entire match falls on his shoulders alone.

Moe feels his heart pound with each step.  He

barely notices the slaps on his back as he walks across the mat. What does catch his eye is the sight of Josh at the end of the team chairs, his head down, drenched in sweat, his teammates trying to console him. The stands are loud with anticipation for this final match and the possible upset. The wrestlers of both teams stand to their feet on each side of the mat. The referee motions to each team to move back and the coaches try to get their boys to take a few steps away so a team point isn't taken away. The cheers begin, "Let's go Moe-o, let's go. Let's go Moe-o...let's go!" Rudi claps his hands furiously but Big Moe doesn't need any encouragement from his coach to get pumped up for this one.

At the whistle, over 500 pounds of beef collide at the center circle. They push and shove like two sumo wrestlers. The referee stops the action quickly as hand fighting turns into slaps in the face and the side of the head.

"Okay fellas, nice and aggressive but you have to keep it legal. Don't DQ yourself."

It's a unique quality to be able to understand the importance and gravity of a match yet not be swept up within it. This ref seems to have things well in hand. He not only sees what's happening on the mat he knows what is happening with the match and the emotions that surrounds the three of the principals involved, the two wrestlers and himself. He starts the match once more and the two boys seem to have listened to his warning and the match continues to be aggressive but clean. Suddenly Big Moe catches a finger in his eye and he pulls away holding his hand to his head. The action stops and Rudi adamantly shouts for a penalty. The ref raises a hand and gives Moe a point. After a short injury time Moe continues with his eye clearly squinting and red. Big Moe starts to force the action now and he takes a grip around the waist of his opponent. With two steps, first his left and then his right foot, he brings his hips close, thrusts his hips out and arches his back and takes his opponent off of the mat and into the air. For s split second the beauty of the moment is undeniable. The crowd freezes for that same moment and watches with awe as Moe elevates his wrestler into the air. The crowd then gasps in unison as the wrestler lands hard on the mat and the referee immediately blows his whistle and raises his finger showing the point he is awarding the thrown wrestler. Slam! Big Moe gets up and slaps his chest with his fist like some primal beast declaring his territory. The match was over and Moe has just lost but looking at the scene it's not clear who the victor would actually be, the loser pounding his chest or the winner writhing in pain on the mat.

The crowd immediately begins jeering the call, more out of disappointment than disagreement. Wrestlers stand with their arms outstretched to display their disbelief. Rudi shouts at the referee as parents yell from the stands. Wrestlers leap to their feet yelling obscenities and the gym seems to be up for grabs. Amidst the chaos Jake sits and watches, unemotional and unnoticed. The combination of disappointment is overcome by his disbelief in the insanity around him. He gets up and half-heartedly joins his teammates in their rant but in the back of his mind he knows the referee's right and can only provide unenthusiastic support for his new team's anger. He stands and hopes no one sees through his feigned support. Just when he was feeling like part of a team, he starts feeling like he's on the outside again.

As the team slowly enters the wrestling practice room the mood is dark and there is no conversation. Coach Rudi walks behind along with the other assistants like cowboys gathering in a herd. There's a feeling of self loathing that comes with a loss like this one. For a team that runs on so much emotion, an upset loss has an even more devastating affect. A coach that has so many demands, unreasonable and otherwise, can have a volatile response to something like this.

"What are you doing? Why are you here if you aren't going to wrestle?"

The anger in his voice seemed to overshadow his accent. His tirade continues and Rudi walks over to Josh Baker.

"You were the turning point Josh. You gave up on that mat today. You put us behind because of it."

Josh looks Rudi straight in the eyes. There's no expression but no real acknowledgment either. Jake looks on and can't help but admire Josh's courage to look the coach straight in the eyes while even the other wrestlers didn't have the stomach to look up. Josh already knew what was coming and had the same hate for himself. Rudi was just hammering in what Josh wanted to hear. He felt the same things but something inside wanted someone to say it out loud. The last thing he wanted was to hear a team mate lie to him and tell him it's okay and that it wasn't his fault.

Jake simply didn't see it that way. "Win as a team and lose as a team" was something that his dad always preached to him at Jackson, but East Temple was different. It doesn't take long before Jake stops hearing the words that come from Rudi and only hears the volume and only recognizes the anger. The words themselves seem to become garbled and incoherent, but even without the recognition of words, the message it pretty clear. This cannot ever happen again.

As the barrage of arrows continued to propel from Rudi's mouth, and some of the anger starts to build within the wrestlers including Jake. There was certainly some resentment to those who should have won but didn't. Success as a team depended on everyone pulling their weight and if that didn't happen, the outcome could turn into this evening's result. After so many hours of sprints, and weights, and drills and torture, to underperform and come up short was enough to dig up anger that may be buried and hidden away. Teams aren't supposed to point the finger at someone, at least that's what you're taught as a kid, but it's hard not to point when the target is being so plainly identified. Don't wave a steak in front of a dog and then tell it not to bite.

Jake understands his new team now, it's ruthless. There is no margin for error or tolerance for failure. It's nothing like Jackson and maybe that's a good thing. After three years at Jackson he still doesn't have a state championship hanging from his bedroom wall. There's been nothing but anticipation followed by disappointment for the past three seasons. There's been plenty of talk about potential but none of it has turned into a championship. Rudi and this East Temple team might just be the thing that's been missing. Maybe he hasn't been ruthless enough, maybe after all the sacrifice and the blood he still has never demanded enough from himself, maybe this is the missing piece to the puzzle, maybe.

The lessons of this day follow Jake into the weekend tournament. Once again Jake finds himself in the finals. Jake is leading 6-2 and has complete control of the match. Jake throws in a leg and pulls back on his opponent's right arm. The referee stands closely by to make sure the arm is in no danger of injury. When Jake pulls it back too far and at an odd angle, the official stops the action to begin again. The referee's whistle only serves to anger Jake as he remembers the ruthlessness he needs to have. When the action resumes, Jake works on the right arm again and takes the arm and drives his head into the upper part of his opponent's armpit in an "arm lever". The pressure on the shoulder becomes great enough that it causes a deep groan of pain from his foe. At the corner of the mat, Coach Rudi cheers encouragement for his wrestler and the take no prisoner's style he is seeing. Jake holds a comfortable lead but can't seem to get the pin. He continues to work on his opponent's arm like a shark that smells blood in the water. By the third period Jake's adversary cannot continue because of the continuous punishment Jake has given. His opponent walks off the mat holding on to his arm that seems to be hanging on by its hinges. He walks to his father and accepts a hug as he winces in pain.

That image hangs in Jake's memory as he sits in his room that night. The first place medal sits on his dresser and Jake stares at it as if he's in a trance, as it mocks him. He sits at the end of his bed and drops his head in his hands, thinking about the way he's wrestled in his most recent matches. He can't understand the lost feeling he has sitting his own bedroom. Just then young James knocks softly on the door.

"Jimmy?"

"Are you up Jake?" as Jimmy peeks his head through.

"You should be sleeping."

"I can't. Let's play XBox!"

Jake can't resist. Besides it'll be a nice distraction. "But we have to be quiet. Mom will get mad at both of us."

As they slip downstairs like a pair of cat burglars, Jake discreetly grabs his new medal.

"Jimmy, go down stairs and get started. I'll bring down some chips and pop."

Young James smiles with excitement as he makes his way to the basement. There's nothing better than to be sneaking around with your older brother. Even if mom catches them, it'll be Jake that gets in trouble since he's the oldest and "should know better", whatever that meant. In the kitchen, Jake takes his first place medal and buries it deep into the trash, hiding it from anyone else who might be throwing something away.

It's a rare Saturday where there is no tournament for the Jackson team. A practice in the morning and then the rest of the day belongs to the wrestlers. It's a day that families appreciate because it's a brief and pleasant break in the middle of such a long grueling season. The afternoon is sunny and crisp but for a January day it's the equivalent of a summer heat wave. Spence takes the opportunity to get an extra workout in at Crooked Hill.

The hill sits alone, almost majestic in its location as it is at the center of the park whose land is completely flat except of course for the hill. The hill is, curiously, perfectly symmetrical and is not crooked in anyway. Today, it serves as an obstacle for Spence to conquer. On a day without an opponent, Spence has decided to defeat this huge mound of dirt. Each sprint up the hill becomes more difficult as Spence pushes himself on a day when others rest. In his mind, he counts down as he nears his goal; five more to go, four more, three, etc. On his last sprint he clinches his fists and stares at the ground as it passes underneath his steps. He digs down into his gut for a little more strength to finish his last trip up the hill. At the top he looks to the sky as if to give thanks to the gods above for the strength to finish. He raises his hands onto his head to help catch his breath and walks in circles and waits for his body to recover.

Spence looks over the tops of the trees and narrows his eyes at the setting sun beaming through the branches. From a distance, you can see the clouds of mist from Spencer's breath and he looks almost majestic atop the conquered hill. He looks down at the world from which he stands atop. That is exactly how he feels, on top of the world. It's something he's never felt before, or at least not that he can remember. With all that he's lost he seems to have gained something. Spence is seventeen and has never lived anywhere else his entire life, and for the first time in as long as he can recall, he feels like he's home. He takes a deep breath and looks around the empty park, the bare trees, his own breath casting shadows at his feet, once again alone, yet without the loneliness.

Dinner at home with mom is now routine and the times when he spent his evenings alone are in the distant past. With Spence wrestling 145 again this season, dinners are brief affairs with small portions and nothing else on the table to reduce the temptation for extra helpings. Janice leaves the food on the stove and she tries to make just enough for the two of them so there isn't a lot of extra calories lying around waiting to be consumed. Making 145 is a bit of a struggle. Spence needs to stay disciplined and not let his weight go up and down. Spence tries to always stay within 5 pounds of his weight. He has eliminated certain foods before the season even started, fast food, pizza, soda, sweetened fruit juices, and he can't remember the last time he had even a single french-fry.

At night he'll retreat into his bedroom and look at the reminders that he has laid out to remind him of both his pride and his purpose. On the wall is the picture of Jon Trenge's wrestling shoes, there are pictures of the Jackson team members in various poses of victory, and there are bracket posters of tournaments he has won. On his dresser sits a few letters from college coaches who are interested in having Spencer join their program. The newest addition of Spencer's room is a calendar. The calendar has each day crossed off like a prisoner awaiting a release date. Spencer's calendar counts down the remaining wrestling season, the last season of his Jackson career. There are two dates circled in thick black marker, one is the date for the state finals, his last chance for a state title. The other box circled is for a tournament in just two weeks, it's a tournament where both the Jackson team and East Temple team will attend.

Trey Davis, with two young children, doesn't like to travel too far away from home for tournaments, but when a team dropped out of the Crimson Clash, he jumped at the opportunity. It's one of the premier tournaments of the season and he knew that Jake and East Temple would be there. It will be a good test for his team and a preview of the 145 match-up that is destined to come, pitting both Jake and Spence in the same bracket.

Jake and Spence haven't spoken to each other since the newspaper article. Now that they have a collision course both in two weeks, and at the end of the season, there won't be any contact. They both feel some of the tensions connected with facing each other on the mat, even though they've rolled with each other since they were six years old. This time, victory means something and so does the defeat.

When Rudi heard that Jackson was going to be at the Crimson Clash, he immediately took Jake aside to let him know. Jake's eye's lit up at the thought of seeing his old teammates again and seeing Coach Davis and of course Spence. The excitement quickly faded when Rudi informed Spence that he is considering having Jake forfeit to Spence if they met in the finals.

The idea was one of strategy. The two are so evenly matched and they know each other so well that it might be better to have their only match up be during the State finals. Rudi wants the changes in Jake's wrestling to be a surprise and not give Spence a chance to learn from a match before the state tournament. The wrestler who wins the first match, at least in Rudi's mind, is at a disadvantage in the next match and it's the next match that is the most important between Jake and Spence. Jake just stared at Rudi, not knowing how to respond at all. It seemed ridiculous, especially with the mindset that his coach has been preaching all year. The East Temple Team wasn't supposed to be afraid of anyone or anything, and here Rudi is telling Jake that he might have to back down from a challenge.

"We'll have to see what happens. Howard might not even be at 145 for this tournament anyway."

Jake just nodded his head and tried to go over Rudi's words once more in his head. He looked at his coach with a glaze over his eyes like a deer staring at a pair of headlights. The chances were good that Spence and Jake would meet in the finals of the Crimson Clash and Rudi may forfeit him. In the back of his head it all just didn't seem right. Avoiding competition was new to him. He tried to understand Rudi's explanation and wanted to believe in him. Jake tried to convince himself that his coach new best. There was also the hope that Spence bumped up to 152 for this one anyway. Many of the Jackson wrestlers have been wrestling at a heavier weight and will be cutting down for the end of the season and the post-season tournaments. Jake knew that Spence might have a hard time staying at 145 and may not even be in the same bracket for the Crimson clash. He had no idea about the circle on Spence's calendar or the conversation Spence had with Coach Davis.

"Wrestling the best is what it's all about. Spence, you should be looking forward to the opportunity to go against Jake." Coach Davis' words are far different from those of Coach Rudi.

"I know coach, I am. I've got the date on my calendar and I'm gonna make the weight."

"That's good to hear. Between you and Jake, it's just a matter of who's having the better match, THAT day. At the end of the day, one of you will walk away with a loss for the season but we're not worried about the W's. We are focused on that top step."

The "top step" that Coach Davis is talking about is the top step of the awards platform for the state title. The most important win is the last one and the most important match is the next one. That's how it's always been coached to him. If you never feel failure, you can never truly succeed. Rudi and his East Temple team was about strategy and getting the edge wherever he could, while the Jackson team has been taught to face any and all challenges and let the chips fall where they may.

Tonight, Sarah Stevens takes her two boys out to

dinner. In the middle of dinner, Sarah pulls out another letter of interest from a College inviting Jake to come for a visit to their campus and to join their wrestling program. Jake's had a few offers but still hasn't made a decision. The Iowa's and the Oklahoma's aren't banging on his door and without a state title, or two or three, they won't be. It is clear however that Jake's wrestling career doesn't have to end at the completion of his senior year.

Spence has also been getting letters of interest and phone calls from coaches. With a few loans here and there, and working every summer, he should be able to swing four years of higher education without too much strain on his mother. There was a time when the thought of wrestling after H.S. was just an idea; a blip in the thought process, but now it's become more and more, a topic that needs to be addressed. It's something that Jake doesn't like to talk about. With his dad around, it was his plan to go away and wrestle somewhere. But now he wants to stay closer to home, closer to his mother and brother. Jake just shakes his head when Sarah pulls out the letter.

"Mom, stop it. I just want to eat in peace." It was said with a smile on his face as his irritation has become a running joke for the family. Sarah would like Jake to stay home as well, but takes pride whenever a letter arrives.

That night, Jake loses himself in his room and stares at the ceiling. Glancing across his walls you would see reminders of Jackson teams of the past. But reminiscing about the past few years are only reminders that the end is just a few weeks away and the last chance that he shares with his long time friend. Getting on the mat with Spence in the next few days may be a look into the future to see who will succeed or fail in that last chance.

# Crimson Clash

There are 16 teams from all areas of the state that have gathered this morning to meet in what is becoming one of the premier tournaments of the season. Wrestlers file out as bus after bus roll up to the gymnasium doors. Parents set up and organize food tables as wrestlers move immediately to the scales. Spence looks around for Jake but the East Temple team is still on the highway.

Weigh-ins are about to begin as the East Temple bus arrives. Wrestlers begin to march into the locker rooms just in time but Spence still doesn't see Jake in his line of wrestlers weighing in at 145. Then he looks across at scale number three and sees Jake lined up with the 152 pounders, he moved up a weight class. Jake catches Spence's eye and just shrugs his shoulders. Spence can only shake his head, hiding both his disappointment and his relief. Both wrestlers are off the hook for now and they both realize it.

After weigh-ins, Jake is warming up in the corner with some of his East Temple teammates. Spence sneaks up from behind and jumps on his back taking Jake to the mat. They roll around for just a few seconds and end up sitting together at the edge of the mat, away from the mass of wrestlers struggling to find warm up space.

"So what's the story fat boy?"

"Coach Rudi had me go up so that we wouldn't meet until states. I'll beat you then." Jake puts on a big smile as he makes that comment.

"That's weak. Don't be afraid to admit if you're scared! With me down here, 152 should go smooth. It'll be you and Sandover in the finals."

"Yeah probably, who's in your bracket?"

Jake gets interrupted by a Mike Fontenetta cradle. Mike scoops up Jakes leg and balls him up to a pin. He releases Jake and now they are going takedowns. Before the two can finish their sparring, coach Rudi calls for all of his wrestlers to take a few laps around the gym to get warm. Mike and Jake embrace, they wish each other luck and Jake jogs off. Without speaking a word, Mike and Spence approach in a wrestling stance and begin to drill.

"Will all wrestlers please clear the mats?!"

As everyone walks off and file into the stands, Jake runs up to Spence and gives him a "pound-hug". This is when two men combine a handshake with a one-armed hug.

"Good luck today."

"Yeah, you too. Come by the table later and see the rest of the guys and Coach Davis."

Coach Davis will always be "Coach Davis" and not just "Coach". "Coach" was Jake's dad.

Jake just nods as he puts on his headphones. It's time to wrestle.

The competition is good and the matches are tight. Mike Fontenetta wins his first two matches but then loses his third on a bad call by the official. Down a point in the third period Mike seemingly takes down his opponent only to have the official wave his hands signaling that the wrestlers are out of bounds and no points are awarded. Thirty seconds later the official is making the same signal again and shaking his head "no" as if to confirm his accuracy to the crowd. Mike shakes his head as if to wonder what he has to do to earn his points. Time runs out on Fontenetta and walks off the mat without his hand being raised. Several wrestlers, from various teams, pat him on the back as he makes his way through the crowd, in recognition of the bad break Mike is trying to swallow.

The rest of his day is spent in the consolation bracket and he coasts to a third place finish. Mike, although disappointed at the result, is satisfied in knowing that he belonged in the final match of a tough bracket today. He knows he's primed for a run at the state title.

Jake bounces in a corner of the gym watching Spence and the other 145's battle in their matches. He knows that they are the opposition he needs to watch for in the next month. Spence looks sharp and as quick as ever. Rudi spies Jake watching the action and tells him how Spence is not as fast as Jake and not as strong. They watch the rest of the match together as Spence dismantles a weaker wrestler. Each move comes with Rudi pointing out apparent flaws in Spencer's wrestling. Jake just nods his head as if he sees the same "weaknesses" that Rudi sees. The truth is that Jake sees his friend at the very top of his game. Spence looks unbeatable and in the back of Rudi's mind, he sees it too.

When Jake takes the mat, Spence moves to a spot in the stands where he can get a clear view. He watches Jake going through his kid like a rag doll. Jake is punishing and more physical than Spence has ever seen. He looks very different from the images Spence recalls of last season. Jake doesn't realize how different his wrestling has become but it's easy to see for Spence. He sits and watches Jake as Coach Davis comes over to join him. Jake shoots a double leg and lifts his man up off the mat. It happens with such perfection, an entire section of the stands give response. Trey Davis' eyes widen and he looks over to Spence.

"He looks good."

Spence just nods.

Coach Davis leans over to remind Spence,

"Everyone can be beat."

Now Spence grins, but never takes his eyes off the mat and never speaks a word.

At 4:00 p.m., the finals are about to begin. The stands are full and spotlights shine on the center mat. Coach Rudi has several East Temple wrestlers vying for a first place as does Jackson H.S. It's been an amazing day of wrestling with many of the top teams around the state competing for the past seven hours. Jake is getting ready for his finals match against Sandover as Spence predicted. He remembers the match Spence had with Sandover and he knows that his strategy will be different. Jake is going to show the wrestling community something about the East Temple version of Jake Stevens. He is tougher but he still has the technique to outclass an opponent. He's not a mauler or a bully on the mat. His game is complete. Wrestlers are warming up and stretching and some spectators can't help but to notice a sight that is seldom seen; two wrestlers from two different teams drilling and warming each other up.

Spence and Jake drill together with precision and timing. Their technique is flawless and spectators, wrestlers and coaches watch in appreciation. Well, not all the coaches. Rudi looks over and the look on his face is clear and easy to read. He didn't want Jake to face Spence in a match and he sure doesn't want them working-out together. Rudi starts to walk over to the mat and grabs an East Temple wrestler on the way. Calling out to Jake, Rudi pushes an East Temple wrestler toward Jake to take Spence's place. Jake looks up and gets the message right away. Feeling like he just got caught with his hand in the cookie jar, he shrugs his shoulders at Spence and begins to workout with his teammate. Just as Spence finds another body to work with and is about to drill with Fontenetta, a voice rings out through the gym for all wrestlers to clear the mats. We are ready to wrestle.

Spence's weight class is first and Jake take a place in the stands along with Coach Rudi for one more scouting session. Spence comes out and begins another impressive display. Spence takes an immediate shot at a low single and lunges at his opponent's ankle, for a quick two point takedown. Rudi nudges Jake's arm as if to ask, "Did you see that?" But Jake is very familiar with everything Spence does on the mat. Rudi leans over and tell Jake, "You neeeed to slow down the pace of the match when you two wrestle. Tie heem aap and make heem wrestle eenside."

Spence dismantles his man like a surgeon; one point after another, one move after another. Rudi sits and looks for weaknesses but Jake knows there aren't any cracks in Spencer's armor. In all the years of wrestling together they've gone back and forth season after season. Neither one has ever consistently been the better. Victory in the practice room has been traded back and forth over the years and in a few weeks they will see who gets to hold on to the victory on the most important stage. While Rudi watches for ways to beat Spence, Jake just watches Spence, with a big part of him wishing he was in a Jackson uniform again. Spence takes an easy decision 12 – 3 and was in complete control of the entire match.

As Spencer's hand is raised, Jake is waiting to step on the mat for his own championship match. When they make eye contact Jake extends his hand and shakes it tilting his hand left and right telling Spence that the performance was only so-so. In response, Spence rolls his eyes with a grin, detectable only to those who know him. But the truth is that Spence looked sharp and Jake knows that his friend is a tough obstacle to the top step.

Meanwhile, Rudi is trying to mend some fences with the official. Coach Rudinoff has had a few occasions to argue a call here and there today. Rudi is the most vocal coach in the gym today, as he is on most days. His arrogance is as recognizable as his accent and a few of the referees are getting tired of his act.

Watching him from the stands, Rudi's demeanor makes him stand out among the masses of wrestlers and coaches. He jumps, yells, and his animated antics make him the most memorable aspect of any tournament. He tries to influence and intimidate referees like he wants his wrestlers to intimidate their opponents. It isn't hard to dislike Rudi's behavior and he makes for an easy villain and so, because of this, the entire East Temple team has taken the role of the villain. The crowd enjoys seeing the East Temple wrestlers lose and will root for anyone who is opposing an East Temple Spartan.

The one exception seems to be Jake. The wrestling community knows Jake and his father. As the end of the season comes closer, people want to see him succeed more and more. He is the lone white hat on a team full of bad guys. Jake steps onto the mat across from Sandover. He remembers the conversation he had with Spence and can feel Spence's eye's on him as he places his foot on the line. He reminds himself of the way he wants to win this match and his feelings after winning his last tournament. Jake doesn't want to feel like he needs to toss another medal in the trash. Finesse is not what Rudi wants to see. Rudi wants to see physical domination from his wrestlers, but more than anything, Rudi wants to win.

Jake proceeds to dismantle Stu Sandover but whenever Jake begins to take command Stu comes back with a reversal or an escape and the match remains close. He hears Rudi yelling and knows he should be putting Sandover away. The ref sees some blood and stops the action. The wrestlers go to their corners and Stu gets his nose worked on. Jake gets some water along with some coaching from Rudi.

"Heee's open for legs. You can throw them een anytime after breakdown. Get da boots een and work him! You mahst be rougher when you are on top. Geeive heem some punishment. Show heem who ees the better wrestler"

Something in Rudi's voice and intensity triggers Jake's adrenaline. He needs to change from his plan of technique and speed to the East Temple style of physical power. Jake nods his head as he swallows from a water bottle. He sees his team mates in the background and notices Spence and the Jackson team watching closely as well. He's the only wrestler with two teams squarely behind him in support. The action starts again and Jake takes his coaches advice and wraps his leg around the leg of Stu Sandover and begins to administer some punishment as Sandover fights Jake's attempts to turn. Jake catches an arm and attempts to pull the arm back for a guillotine. Jake tries to work the arm back but fails. He thrusts his hips into him and drives Stu forward and works his arm again. This time Jake gets control and Jake can feel that he has him. Jake cranks the arm higher and Stu winces in pain and fights to get his arm back under his own control. With another jerk of the arm Stu's shoulder goes into a dangerous position and the ref blows the whistle to stop the action. "Potentially dangerous" is the call and the wrestlers need to start the action anew.

Jake throws his leg in again and goes to the same arm and begins to crank for the guillotine. Jake pulls harder and hears the warnings of the referee to "keep it safe", but once again the action is stopped for the safety of Stu's shoulder. As the action re-starts for the third time Rudi yells out to the ref to, "Let them wrestle".

By now the referee has had enough. Listening to Rudi argue throughout the day had run its course. He stops the action and charges Coach Rudinoff with an unsportsmanlike conduct and a team point is taken away from the East Temple Spartans. Another violation would result in Rudi being removed from the tournament. The move seems to have the desired affect, as Coach Rudi sits down quietly in his seat and broods like a child taking a time-out. Looking closely at the crowd you can see smiles and some others in the stands giving applause.

Jake ignores the commotion and remains in the center of the mat waiting to wrestle again. When they begin again, Jake ends up with both his legs wrapped around Snadover's waist and he begins to squeeze mercilessly. The referee raises his hand again but this time it's to give a point to Sandover and Jake is hit with a penalty.

The referee offers some explanation along with

advice. "No Jake, you can't just wrap your legs around and punish. You're not working the move."

Jake can only squeeze his eyes shut in disbelief. Sandover walks over to his corner and a trainer comes to take a look as he moves his arm in circles trying to work some pain out from his shoulder and now his ribs.

The lost point doesn't hurt Jake and in the third period Stu is worn down enough that Jake takes over with a comfortable 5 point lead.   He coasts to a comfortable victory and as Jake's hand is raised, his eyes find Spencer signaling the same so-so hand gesture that Jake gave him. Spence knows he's in for a rough match with Jake and sees a Jake Stevens that's more aggressive, and with a style that borders on being malicious.

As the fans and wrestlers wander out into the parking lots, Jake feels a hand on his shoulder. It's Trey Davis.  As soon as Jake turns to see, they both embrace without a word.  Jake was avoiding him most of the day because he just didn't know what to do when he saw him. It was too uncomfortable, it was simply too sad.

"We miss you son."

Maybe it was the word "son" that set all the emotions flowing. There were no words that could escape Jake's throat as they both held back tears and emotion.  It was like an extension of the funeral and they were both mourning their loss once more.  As they pulled apart and both wiped some tears from their eyes, Trey smiled like a proud father.

"The door is always open son.   Remember, we are still your family."

"I know coach, thanks"

"Ok, take care of yourself and I guess I'll see you at State's"

The bus ride home is a quiet one.  The long day started at Jackson H.S. at 5 a.m. in order to get to weigh-ins on time. Wrestling started at 9:30 and the last final match ended just before 6 p.m. A single match may only last 6 minutes but a tournament is a marathon affair. Coach Davis notices Spence staring out the window, seemingly deep in thought.

"I know you're tired, you should get some sleep."

"Did you see Jake today? He looked really good."

"No better than you Spence. He'll try to bang your head and go at you real hard. You just have to expect it and take what he gives you. It is time though."

"Time for what?"

"Time to step it up"

Monday at practice the Jackson team has a guest in the room. Bernard Miles knows Trey Davis from their ties to wrestling in the Chicago area. Miles went on to wrestle in the national arena and has travelled all over the world competing in freestyle tournaments in Russia, Germany, and the Far East. He even had a brief stint taking advantage of his skill to find some success fighting MMA in the sport's infancy. Even though he was successful fighting in the cage, punching someone until he was bloody or knocked out just wasn't his cup of tea. Today he runs his own catering business with his wife and daughters. In the winter he helps at his daughter's high school's wrestling team and has never had a season away from the sport. At Trey's request, Bernard is here to help the Jackson team prepare for the post season and to also have Bernard teach Trey's wife the secret to the Miles' family pot roast.

The rest of the team works their regular practice while Bernard and Spence quietly work in the corner. It starts with Miles telling Spence to wrestle him like Jake will be wrestling. Spence smiles and starts to bang and maul. He snaps and clubs the head, his hands are like anvils when they land on Miles. Spence beats on him until he decides to take an attack at a single leg and Bernie sprawls and counters to a fresh start on their feet. This

time Bernie stays a bit further away.  When Spence comes
in to pound again, Bernard suddenly disappears from
view, and Spence finds himself with his legs wrapped up
and giving up the takedown.

"Watch Jake and see if he gets sloppy with his ties.
Most guys will relax when they think they're able to bully
you and they will snap you right down to their legs.  The
best time is right after a leg attempt and he comes to
engage again.  You came into me thinking you could just
pound me again and planning your next attack."

Spence just nodded his head, still amazed at how
fast Miles was in on him.  For the rest of the practice they
worked on ways to use Jake's aggressive style to his
advantage.  Bernard showed Spence a few moves in
combination to take advantage of Jake's habit of lifting
opponents off his legs.  Spence began to perfect a
transition from a single leg into a hip toss and a double leg
transitioning right into an arm throw.  Some of the Jackson
wrestlers watched and began working on the same
combinations with great success and Trey would begin to
see dividends of Bernard Miles' visit the very next
weekend.  Some of the Jackson wrestlers took to the
instruction like fish to water and the new technique was
displayed on several occasions.  But Spence would keep
his new arsenal under wraps, preferring to continue to
seek its perfection in the wrestling room.  Working the
move here and there against weaker competition would
not be the same as hitting it on Jake Stevens.  Spence knew
it would take some time before he could bring it to a big
time match.

Spence knows that one of the keys to beating Jake
was going to be working with as many different quality
partners as he could.  Working with Coach Miles, Ortega,
Carlson, Fontenetta and the others in the room was a good
start.

Jake on the other hand had Coach Rudi to roll
with each day.  Rudi had a unique way of becoming a

different person on the mat and could change styles like changing headgear. He could lead and shoot with either leg, he hits a single and a high crotch to either side and could finesse or muscle to suit his needs. Jake had never seen a wrestler so complete, and he knew that Rudi could take him to the top step.

After practices, Coach Rudi had Jake and several others do an extra workout session in the weight room. It was a power routine that consisted of jumping on boxes, lifting tractor tires, swinging medicine balls and climbing ropes. The weight wasn't heavy but the sets were intense. The workouts lasted all of 20 minutes but in Rudi's mind, those extra few minutes made the difference between second and third, between first and second, between gold and silver.

With just a few weeks left in the season Spence has reached another gear and is running on all cylinders like he never has before. Sometimes an athlete gets into such a groove that the speed around him seems to occur in slow motion. That is the place where Spence currently resides. He's untouchable. He wrestles in a rhythm and a flow that displays an almost clairvoyant anticipation of his opponent. Even when wrestling top competition, Spence seems to be several classes above and contenders become relegated to beaten "also-rans" in the wake of Spencer Howard. Janice Howard has agreed to put the college decision on the shelf for the time being and has made her plans for the State tournament; vacation days are arranged and her hotel room is already booked.

Sarah Stevens has adjusted to her new situation and embraces the closeness of her family. Her sisters are a comfort and it feels good to be around so many who will watch over you. She sees less of Jake these days. He comes home and spends much of his time sleeping and allowing his body to have some much needed rest. Jake never worked so hard and been so unrelenting in his workouts and practices. He sits quietly at the dinner table with little to say. Young James does most of the talking at the dinner table these days and Jake does his best to not be annoyed at his brother's constant chatter. Jake will stare at his plate and hate that so much noise around the table has to do with absolutely nothing. He would like nothing more than to just tell Jimmy to shut up but can't deal with the hassle that a comment like that would stir from his mother.

Sarah makes a few subtle attempts to pry some conversation out of Jake but she knows not to push too hard. She can recognize the effort Jake's putting in and the exhaustion that he carried from day to day. She understands that it's Jakes last chance to reach his goal. She knows that the last thing she wants her son to carry with him are the thoughts of what could have been. Jake understands that he needs to finish his final high school season with no regrets and no questions unanswered. For Jake, there will be no "what ifs" or "I wish I hads". Jake is putting everything he has out there and in a few weeks he'll find out if all he has will be enough.

The first day of the district tournament passes in the routine Spence is accustomed to. He breezes through the first day and feels full of energy even with the new rules Coach Davis has set for him. Today, Spence is not allowed to pin. In an effort to give Spence as much work as he can get, Coach Davis has instructed Spence to score points and "get some work in". Spence is to go the whole 6 minutes or win by a technical fall. All day long Spence was busy scoring points in his matches. He would release his opponent after taking him down and would work different escapes from the bottom. Some of the parents thought that Spence was being unsportsmanlike-like but the other coaches in the room understood what was going on. After each match Spence would quickly shake hands and run off to do some sprints in the hall. In years past, the purpose would be to get in more conditioning but this time it has an additional purpose. After a while he tires of hearing congratulations as he's comes off the mat, especially when words of encouragement are coming from people he hardly knows: coaches, assistant coaches, parents, and even referees. The sprints let him escape and run away from the admiration and the pressure.

Not surprisingly, Jake's day on the other side of the state goes much like Spencer's. However, Rudi's instructions are far different from Coach Davis. Jake tries to plow through each wrestler that gets in his way like a steamroller. Jake pins his way through the first day and expends more energy during his after match sprints than during the matches themselves. Rudi is quick with praise and has great pride in his new addition to the team. Jake wrestles three times and spends less than six minutes wrestling the entire day. Weak competition and an insane intensity combine for a quick day for Jake.

Day two is a bit tougher and that is part of the reason for Jake wasting no time in dismissing his previous opponents. Today, he has two tough matches but he is fresh and ready to go since his first day of the tournament was so easy. Although the last two matches are against quality opponents and both matches go the distance, there is still little doubt as to the outcomes. The district tournament is merely a formality and Jake steps onto the top step of the stand and collects his 4th district title.

With both Spencer and Jake moving on to their Regional Tournament with such ease, it dawns upon newspaper reporter, Tim Decker that there is quite a story to be told about these two old friends who have both lost their fathers, their coach, and are both on a direct collision course ending on the state title mat. Decker calls both the East Temple and Jackson Coaches and asks permission to come and interview the boys. Rudi welcomes Decker with open arms and shines up the pictures in his office and gives his silver medal another polish.  A few hours before Decker is to arrive Rudi calls Jake into his office and informs him of the interview.

"Coach, what are you talking about?  I don't want to talk to any reporter!"

"Jake, trahst mee.  Eet ees good for da program and can be a way to honor your father and remind everyone of the man he was.  Peeple want to know about you and Spencer.  Eet eesn't often the wrestling gets this amount of press een da paper.  Eet is good for everyone in de sport."

Well, he was right about that.  There are still people at East Temple who think wrestling is what they see on the cable channels with the muscle bound maniacs jumping off the ring posts.  At the same time he knows that Rudi relishes the thought of being in the papers and reading anything about himself.  He speaks about publicizing the sport but Jake knows how much Rudi wants this for himself too.

"Ok coach, as long as my mom says it's alright."

Decker arrives as practice is just about winding down.  Like many high school sports reporters he knows little about wrestling but marvels at what he sees as he enters the practice room.  The fog and the heat, along with the pools of sweat make an interesting first impression.  He watches and takes notes and it isn't until his second page of notes that a coach or a wrestler even realizes this neophyte is in the room.  After practice, Decker and Jake move down the hall to escape to the coolness of the cafeteria for the interview.   Jake has spoken to reporters before but never for such a big feature.  A few weeks before his 18th birthday he still finds himself tongue-tied from time to time.  He breaks into a new sweat but this is not from his workout but from nervousness.

"What's it like to be wrestling for a new team and a new coach?"

"I miss the guys at Jackson.  I mean I grew up

with those guys and I've wrestled with some of them since I was just a little kid. But East Temple has been great. The guys here accepted me right away."

"And what about your new coach?"

"Coach Rudi is tough. I've always been coached by my dad, so it's been a different experience for me.....a good one." The words are forced out of his mouth.

Then Decker asks a question with the finesse of a wily veteran reporter. Giving Jake the room a teenager might need and the respect a surviving son deserves.

"Would you like to tell me some things about your dad?"

Jake pauses for a moment and remembers what Rudi said about honoring his father.

"Yeah, I would. He was the best. I miss him a lot and I know the guys at Jackson miss him too. He was a great coach and everyone knew him. He taught me everything I know about wrestling and I owe him everything. He died in a car accident last year, just before the state tournament. I want to win this state title for him."

"What are your thoughts about possibly meeting Spencer Howard for the state title?

"Probably? There's no question that it'll be him and me. Spence is my best friend but I'm gonna beat him."

"How do you know?"

With a laugh, "I just do."

When Trey Davis spoke with Decker he referred him to Janice Howard and Spence. Spence wasn't sure about the interview either but said okay when Decker told him that Jake was in. The interview took place at the Howard home with Janice making some finger sandwiches for the occasion. They sat and exchanged a few pleasantries of small talk in the living room. Spencer seemed at ease and ready when Decker started in by saying, "So, shall we get started?"

With that Janice excused herself to the kitchen and began cleaning up, keeping an ear pointed directly toward the living room all the while.

"Spence, what do you think about possibly wrestling Jake Stevens in a couple of weeks?"

"It's going to be a great match. Jake's a tough wrestler and he's having a great season."

"How has the new coaching staff been this season?"

"Well, Coach Davis isn't new. He's been with Jackson for a while and he's always been one of my High School coaches. We all miss Coach Stevens. I think Coach Davis misses him as much as anyone. Coach Stevens was friends with my dad and when he died, Coach Stevens kindof took his place. He was like my second dad"

"So that makes you and Jake…brothers?"

"Absolutely."

"Will it be hard to try and beat your 'brother'?"

"No, I'm looking forward to it. It'll be all smiles at first but when we step on the mat it'll be all business."

"And if you lose?"

"I won't lose. Ok, Ok…if I lose at least my best friend will have won a state title."

But with that last statement Spence shrugs his shoulder and his smile suddenly disappears. The thought of losing isn't something that sits well with him and the gracious thing is to feel good about Jake but the reality is that losing just isn't something he's ready to even think about.

"Do you have a plan on how to beat Jake? You guys have been wrestling each other all your lives."

"Sure I have a plan, maybe a few tricks up my sleeve too. But Jake will be reading this right??" And with that Spencer's smile returns and Decker laughs with a nod of his head.

As part of his article, Decker would write:

*In just a few weeks there will be a moment of time that will climax the high school careers of two terrific young men. They both seek a prize that has eluded them and a mere six minutes will determine who will succeed in the quest that has taken a lifetime of pursuit. At the end of those six minutes there will be one who will not have his hand raised but they will both stand together in triumph. Congratulations Jake and Spencer, you are both champions.*

# Regionals Senior Year

Another Regional tournament and Jake wishes he could hide from the memorial that is to be given in his father's honor. This year's outstanding wrestler of each of the state's Regional Tournaments will receive a trophy named the "David Stevens Outstanding Wrestler Award". Before the National Anthem a speaker recalls for the audience, that it was right after last year's Regional Tournaments that Coach Stevens was lost in a car accident. Looking around the gym, Jake is conspicuously absent from the floor. He stands with his head down in a corner of the gym behind the stands and out of view from as many people as possible.

He hears that the outstanding wrestler award will be in honor of his father and a rush of blood flows through his veins and he suddenly feels warm and numb. Jake knows that the award will be his as long as he wins and takes an expected first place. Heck they'll probably give it to him even if he loses in the first round. It would feel like charity either way. This is too much. He just wants to wrestle. Now he has to dominate the tournament to make sure that he's deserving of the award bearing his father's name.

During his first match of the day he comes out in almost a panic. Right off the whistle he takes a bad shot and ends up losing the first takedown of the match. He immediately escapes and charges again only to end up butting heads with this opponent. Both wrestlers recoil backward and the referee stops the action and sends both wrestlers to their coaches. Rudi is saying something to Jake but nothing is penetrating. He just stands there waiting for the bells to stop ringing in his head.

When the action starts again Jake can feel the frenzied pace of the action and decides to try a move he saw several years ago at a summer camp. It's one of the most impressive moves on the mat, the "super-duck". Jake half lunges to one side and as his opponent reacts, Jake changes direction and ducks around to the opposite side of his opponent. When done to perfection, a wrestler will get his takedown without even touching his opponent. It was a thing of beauty and demonstrated shear dominance of technique over an opponent. It was like shooting your free throws left handed or hitting a home run with one arm. Jake pushed and snapped and moved in and out measuring his chance for the move. One fake, two fakes, then bang – "super-duck"!!

The crowd that saw the move "Ahhh-ed" in appreciation as the rest of the crowd scorned themselves for missing it. The rest of the match went by quickly as Jake finished his sloppy start with a pin in the second period. The only thing that will be remembered about the match will be Jake hitting his first "super-duck" in competition. Putting on that performance makes Jake feel like some of the pressure has been taken off his shoulders. He needed to be dominant or spectacular today. With that first match he's well on his way.

Across the state Spencer is wrestling to win a David Stevens Trophy of his own. This Eastern Regional is the toughest in the state and there are several blue chippers in the gym today. There are more state champs, state placers, and previous state qualifiers at this regional than any other in the state. The choice of outstanding wrestler is up for grabs and wrestlers would best be advised to concentrate on surviving rather than having delusions of dominating. That is the message that Trey Davis gives his wrestlers before the wrestling begins. Each one of them would like to win the award that bears the name of their former coach and the sentimental vote would naturally go to a Jackson wrestler, but they are going to have to win first.

Spencer wins methodically but not in spectacular fashion. The star of the first day is Fontenetta who has upset two state placers who stood in his way. Actually, most coaches recognized that Mike Fontenetta's wins were hardly upsets but since Mike didn't even wrestle in last year's post-season tournaments the wins stood out as the matches of the day. Spencer's mind was split between his matches and his weight. He needed to make sure he won and moved on to the second day but he also had to make weight for the second day as well. Sucking down to the 145 class wasn't too difficult but doing it 2 days in a row for the second straight week was a bit harder. He didn't mind going the extra period today because it would help him to make weight for tomorrow. He does his sprints after his matches but didn't want to do too many extra and not have enough energy for his next match. He watched what he ate and drank all afternoon long and when his last match was over for the day, he started to run the halls.

Of course all the wrestlers making the second day have to make weight and Spencer has plenty of company as footsteps echo through the hallways and wrestlers go about the business of being wrestlers.

"Spence! Wait up!"

Spence recognized the voice right away. It was John Kim, his friend from youth wrestling and the guy who took Vance Tolliver's last chance at a state title. They fall into step with one another. They go through the normal wrestler small talk and tell each other how much weight needs to be lost and then they each talk about the matches of the day and matches of tomorrow. After about 10 minutes the only thing they share is company. They are lock step with one another but hardly a word is spoken as they each take on the task of sweating down some weight.

"Ok Spence, that's it for me. I should be good. Good luck tomorrow."

With that, John Kim jogs his way down to the lockers and Spence is alone again among 5 or 6 other wrestlers in the halls. He feels the sweat dripping off his face and can tell that his shirt is getting sufficiently soaked. He'll make the weight easily for tomorrow but feels the need to keep going. It's the end of a tournament that all began about nine hours ago and Spence is still full of energy. He keeps running.

At the same time, several counties away, Jake goes through the same routine. He's running just to run. There's no real weight issue, he merely doesn't want to go home just yet. There hasn't been too many challenges on the mat today and the running helps to clear his head. He doesn't want to go home, he doesn't want to listen to Rudi, and he doesn't want to answer any questions or exchange any pleasantries with the fans in the stands or his teammates. Right now he needs to be alone and just listen to the rhythm of his own footsteps.

Day two begins with Jake taking control with a quick takedown as he ducks under his opponent's arm with such ease that it's as if they both choreographed it for the crowd. On top, Jake has become simply punishing. It has become a trademark of East Temple wrestling. Every wrestler on the team will lace in their legs to completely dominate while in the top position. Jake cranks on the wrestler's neck and pries on his shoulder time and time again. Jake may not be gaining anything in points but he is surely winning the battle of wills. As the punishment continues it's as though he is taking away the spirit of his adversary. With the score 9 -1 in the third period there is no doubt as to the outcome and Jake coasts to an easy victory and is well on his way to a regional title and earning the award that bares his father's name.

Spencer's day is a bit tougher. His first match of the day will be with Darren Takashi, the wrestler who beat Jake last year at the State tournament. Darren spent the summer alternating between Judo tournaments and wrestling tournaments. Spence knows he will have his hands full. Anyone who can hand Jake a loss is someone to worry about.

Spence has been trying to remember the match with Jake but since it was right after the accident he draws a blank. He knows Takashi is dangerous on his feet so he knows to be cautious when he's going for a takedown. The first period is slow as Takashi and Spence wrestle as if any mistake they make can cost them the match. All eyes are focused on their match. It's generally agreed that this should have been the final match at 145 but the two just happened to draw each other one round earlier. During the first period dance, both wrestlers are warned for stalling with both coaches expressing equal amounts of displeasure. Trey Davis sits in his corner trying to remain calm and not give away his concern. He calls out to Spence to, "Beat him on the mat"

This comment might seem confusing to those unfamiliar with the sport but Spence knows just what his coach is telling him. They wrestled evenly on their feet but now that they are wrestling off of their feet, it's time for Spence to take charge. Takashi takes the down position and will try to get away for a point and then go back to work on his feet. Spence needs to turn him and score.

On the whistle, Spence stops Takashi's first move and wraps up Takashi's waist. Spence changes to a ride he learned from Coach Miles. He slips his left knee under Takashi, grabs a far ankle, and drapes over him waiting for him to react. Darren Takashi sits back, posts his leg to free his ankle and takes the bait. Spence crunches him down reaching one hand over Takashi's head and the other hand under his far leg and scoops Takashi into a "cradle". Spence rocks him back quickly and gets a fast 5 count from the referee, and takes a three point lead.

Darren breaks out of Spence's grip and shakes his head for a moment, mad at himself for getting caught in Spencer's trap. Spencer dominates Takashi for the rest of the period. Spence throws in a leg wrapping his left leg around the left leg of Takashi. After Spence breaks Takashi down flat he begins to turn him for a few more points before the end of the period. Time is running out in the second and the score remains 3-0. Spence can't seem to turn Darren but with 10 seconds left in the period Takashi tries to free himself but Spence is a split second faster and catches Takashi's head with his forearm and brings Takashi to his back for 2 more quick points.

In a rare loss of composure, Spence gets himself just the slightest amount out of position as he tries for a pin and finish Takashi off. Darren takes advantage and scrambles for a reversal to salvage some points and keep the match within distance at 5-2.

The third period begins with Takashi on top. Off the whistle he tries to quickly tilt Spence to expose his back to the mat. Darren's coach stands to his feet, shouts something to the ref and holds his hands up in the air. The referee shakes his head letting all those watching know that there are no points awarded. Several parents jump to their feet and shout to the referee and much of the crowd expresses their displeasure as well. Spence gets back to his stomach and realizes that the crowd is against him. Like always, wrestling fans revel in witnessing the upset. The whole idea of an upset is to have the lesser combatant win over the more accomplished and talented. The assumption is that the winner "went for it" or he "rose to the occasion" and performed beyond his own expectations. When you see an upset on the mat the idea is that the loser didn't work hard enough or got lazy and the victor has broken through because of his own tremendous preparation. The truth is seldom close to either of these two extremes.

Spence can barely hear the crowd as he frantically works to stay off his back. Suddenly, he feels Takashi release his pressure and lets him go, giving up a point to wrestle back on their feet. It's 6-2 and Takashi has just over a minute to score 5 points to pull out the match. Spence knows Takashi is a master at throwing people to their backs. Staying away will cost him a point since he already has a stalling warning on him. Darren presses the action and Spence tries to keep his hips down and push away from Darren's grip. The referee points a finger to the sky and awards a point to Takashi penalizing Spence for stalling. The action goes out of bounds and the referee warns Spencer to keep wrestling. Spence looks over to the corner and Coach Davis just motions for Spence to stay low and shoot at Takashi's legs.

Spence takes a few extra steps to get back to the circle and catches his breath. He's not tired. He just wants to take a second to gather his thoughts. He stops to ask the referee the score, but Spence knows exactly what the score is. The question is asked in order to get a few more seconds to slow things down and take away some of the momentum that Takashi is riding.

"You are up 6-3 and there is 48 seconds left in the match. Here we go…wrestle!"

Takashi comes in fast trying to make Spence wrestle upper body and find an opportunity to execute one of his Judo throws. Spence can't give up another stalling point and bring the match within 2 points. Spence takes a low single leg shot and grabs the heel of Takashi's lead foot. Darren fights to counter and Spence scrambles to finish his takedown and seal the win. Trey Davis tries to call out to instruct Spence and keep an eye on the clock all at the same time. In the stands, Janice Howard yells out to Spence as if she might have the slightest chance of being heard from the third row and over the hundreds of voices in the gym. The one voice that seems to be heard above all the other shouting finally comes through loud and clear for every interested party. "Two takedown!"

Spence looks up at the score and sees 8-3 with time running down closer and closer to zeroes. The buzzer sounds and there is no display of emotion on

Spencer's face. He shakes hands with Darren Takashi, has his hand raised by the referee and then picks up his warm-up and runs out of the gym to run a few sprints.

Jake is getting ready for his finals match and is more than ready to go. It seems like he's been waiting forever for the consolation matches to finish and his body is getting tired from all the nervous energy he's been expending. The waiting and the anticipation of wrestling will often drain a young man. Nerves and anxiety can take a real toll on an athlete. Sometimes a wrestler can get worn out before he even steps out onto the mat. Jake is so anxious to get on the mat that he warms up two matches earlier than usual and by the time his match is close to begin, he's lost his sweat and is cooling down. Recognizing the problem, Coach Rudi rolls with Jake on a nearby practice mat to get him warmed up again.

Jake's opponent watches from a distance and bounces up and down in readiness for the match. Gene Thompson is a sophomore who survived two overtime matches to get to the finals match with Jake. Gene's coach didn't expect him to place in the top 4 and here he is wrestling for a first place and is already guaranteed a trip to the State Finals Tournament. He happened to be in the right place at the right time this weekend. His last opponent injured a shoulder and could not continue his match with Thompson. The match before that, Thompson benefitted from an opponent who was weakened by a flu bug. The matches before were overtime victories that could have gone either way. Gene Thompson was indeed very fortunate this weekend but now he had to face Jake Stevens and he knew that his luck was about to run out.

The tournament director announces the start of the 145 pound match and Jake and Thompson make their way to the mat. Rudi follows right behind as Jake leads the way. Jake checks in and turns to his coach. Rudi says a few words with his thick Russian accent and gives Jake a hard slap on each side of Jake's face. It's time to up the intensity and focus. The slaps get Jake's blood going and hopefully helps to get his body back in gear.

From the start of the whistle it's clear that Thompson cannot stay with Jake and the difference in ability is painfully obvious to all in observance. Regional Finals matches are rarely this lopsided but Jake begins to dismantle Gene with ease. Jake comes out with such energy and intensity that some are fearful for the safety of Thompson. Thompson seems to have resided himself to his fate and is satisfied with getting as far as second place and going to the state tournament for the first time. Rather than attacking Jake, Thompson is busy making sure he is not injured in the match.

After only three and a half minutes Jake pins and the match is over. He is able to allow himself to wind down. Jake pinned his way through most of the tournament with only one match going the entire 6 minutes. At the end of the awards the "David Stevens Most Valuable Wrestler" award is given out. There isn't a person in the gym that doesn't recognize who the award will be given too and the spectators are all ready to stand to their feet in recognition.

*"Last season the sport of wrestling lost one of its greatest coaches, one of its greatest participants, one of its greatest friends. David Stevens was an ambassador for the sport and was an example of all that wrestling should be. He left behind not only a great legacy but also a team, a family, and a community that will always remember him. It is with great honor that I present the David Stevens Most Valuable Wrestler award to his son, Jake Stevens."*

Listening to those words was harder than any match he had the last two days. Jake's eyes turned red and glassy as he walked to the center of the mat to accept his prize. Sarah stands at the center of the mat holding the plaque named for her husband, and ready to present it to her son. The tears in his eyes make it hard for Jake to see the crowd on their feet celebrating the moment. When Sarah embraced a tearful Jake she could only say, "I love you" and squeezed him like she'd never get another chance to hold him again. She squeezed so hard that it snapped Jake out of his emotional state and laughed at how he was getting abused by his own mother.

"Take it easy mom, you're hurting my ribs!"

Jake then turned to the crowd and waved a grateful "thank you". He thought to himself that maybe it's over now. Maybe it was time to move on and allow the past to be in the past. Maybe the pain will start to fade away. He couldn't be sure of any of that but he did know that he had one more week and one final shot at finishing what he started.

# The Last Chance

There won't be any phone calls this weekend between Jake and Spence. They'll both see each other soon enough and there really isn't much to say. Besides, Coach Rudi has specifically told Jake not to have any contact with Spence until the tournament, and even then Rudi wants conversations to be limited. In Rudi's mind, they are not to be friends until after the match and after Jake has won his title.

With just a few days away from the state tournament, Janice Howard takes time to reminisce about the past few years. She takes out a few scrapbooks and other artifacts that recall some of the memories that have filled their lives. There are medals, and trophies, and newspaper clippings. There are certain gaps in her memory during the years she spent working 12 hour days and missed so much of Spencer's matches. During those seasons, Spence would come home and tell her all about his matches and Janice would visualize each match in her head as he spoke. So now, looking back at past seasons, there are moments when Janice isn't quite sure if her memories are real or imagined. Regardless, she holds each memory dearly, and looking back she smiles to herself as she wipes a tear from her eye.

Spencer is spending his Sunday afternoon at the YMCA where he and fellow Regional Champion Mike Fontenetta are trying to ease their aches and pains with the heat of a sauna. They are both feeling the effects of two tough weeks of wrestling. Spence is nursing a sore shoulder and a knee that has been flaring up all season long.

"Are you hurtin' bad?"

"Not too bad. The knee is kindof swollen but it's the shoulder that really bothers me. What's up with you?"

"I'm just aching from the usual spring time soreness. I don't think Coach Rollins appreciates me wrestling. He's been asking me about my health for the last two weeks."

When Fontenetta injured an elbow his sophomore year he lost velocity in his throwing arm and stopped pitching for the Jackson High baseball team and moved to second base. Coach Rollins never said anything about not wrestling but Mike just had a sense about it. He's heard the football coach tell his guys to not wrestle because he was afraid of injuries and all the weight cutting. What football coaches don't understand is that wrestlers lose fat and become a better conditioned, and tougher, athlete when they wrestle. Besides, it doesn't take long for a wrestler to pack on the pounds again.

"So is Jake gonna be on your side of the bracket?"

Mike knew the answer to the question, but didn't know how else to open the topic. The rest of the Jackson team was looking forward to seeing the match up.

"Nope. I won't see him till the finals. He looked pretty good at the Crimson Clash. It's gonna be tough. He's not the same wrestler he was a year ago"

"Neither are you. Don't worry, you'll wear him out. Hey, who's coming to workout with us tomorrow?"

"Coach Miles and Ortega, but not sure if anyone from other teams are coming."

With Fontenetta, Spence, Miles, and Ortega: Spence and Mike will have a very good workout group to prepare for next week. Along with 140 and 145, Jackson is bringing their 171,189, and 215 pound wrestlers to the state tournament. The lone light weight will be at 119 where Vince Vitulli will need a practice partner to prepare for the big dance. With 6 wrestlers moving on to the state tournament, Coach Davis is pleased but still thinks two others could have made it to the final week if they had a break here or there.

"So do you know where you're going yet?"

Fontenetta was one of 10 top finalists in last years "Mr. Baseball" award that goes to the top player in the state.

"Yeah, I'm gonna stay with my aunt and go to Southern Illinois. It'll be a "partial" (scholarship) but I won't be living on campus so money won't be too bad. I might try walking on the wrestling team. What about you?"

Spence has heard this same question for over a year and he's never really had an answer for anyone. He never thought much past high school and his grades were evidence of that thought process. Academically, Spencer has always been in the middle part of the curve and stood comfortably near the 50th percent of Jackson high graduating class. Spence always figured he'd go to work somewhere and just keep coming to the Jackson High wrestling room for as long as they'd let him. But in the past year there has been plenty of interest from colleges hoping to snag him for their squad. Even without a state title, Spence has made coaches take notice.

"I've gotten a few calls from one of Tommy's coaches at Arizona. I think he must be talking up the Jackson program. I think I'm gonna stay close to home though, going away would be too much money, I think."

Jake, on the other hand, has always had his sights on wrestling in college. His dad did, and his parents have always emphasized the need to go to college even if he didn't wrestle. There was a time when he figured that he'd be going to school with Spence, but now he had no idea what was going to be in store for him next year. At the moment he really didn't care. Tonight he's going through a Sunday night technique session with Rudi.

The few East Temple wrestlers who survived the Regional tournament have gathered for a short wrestling session. They'll work on technique for about an hour and go over some finer points that Rudi noticed from the matches. The action is more like boxers sparring. They get a chance to work some soreness out of their muscles and also try to improve upon their technique at the same time. On this rare occasion, there is no live wrestling in the East Temple room but there is some wrestling going on. With the state tournament now just a few days away, Rudi would like each wrestler to live on the mat if he could make them.

For the two favorites to win the 145 title, the Monday sunrise provides some needed light for their morning run. Neither Spence nor Jake wants to walk into the room today heavy. They are hundreds of miles apart but their routines this morning are the same; bundle up, drink some water, grab a bagel, and hit the road. They both start by running into the sun so that the brighter sunlight will be at their backs for the return jog. The music blaring through their earphones help to shut out all the distractions from their outer surroundings as well as storms that are churning within them.

Early in the run the mind wanders and thoughts race in and out of their consciousness. Flashes of the past and visions of the future bounce back and forth with each step. Pictures of standing on the top step, images of a raised hand in triumph, remembrances of past disappointments, and reminders of the opponent that you will face rattle through their heads with each step of the pavement. The more they think the more they doubt. They wonder if they can win and the fear of failure sneaks its way into their mind. In the wrestling room, where there is always a task to focus upon and goal to be achieved, thoughts of failure remain suppressed. On a lonely road where there is little else but your own footsteps to accompany you, all the "what ifs" come out of the shadows and are brought to light.

On the last part of the run, as fatigue begins to take over, the same "what if" occurs to both Jake and Spence. What if I didn't work hard enough? Some doubts and fears can drive you to succeed. What if doing one more mile will give me that edge?

They each run past their houses and push farther then planned. They both seek the point of failure where they cannot go any longer. Their paces pick up and they both race to find that point where there is nothing more left in them to give. The answer to the question, "How much is enough?" is…"Everything."

As Jake enters into the arena, the smell of new wrestling mats fill his senses and he walks across one to feel the cushion under his feet. It doesn't take long before he is just one among a mass of state qualifiers from all around the state and space on the mat quickly becomes a valued commodity.  From the 103 pound freshman to the 275 pound veteran senior, the diversity of the athletes is clear to see. The vast differences not only can be witnessed in their stature but in their demeanor as well. While some lie on the mat calm and restful, others are wound up tight and can only burn off their energy by jogging around the mats, jumping rope or wrestling in a small section of a crowded mat. The final difference that separates the competitors is far more difficult to recognize. Spence can see it all too clearly, as he makes his way around the mats mingling with long time friends and former opponents.

The author Herman Melville said that "the eyes are the gateway to the soul".

G.K. Chesterton wrote, "There is a road from the eye to the heart that does not go through the intellect."

The truth of these musing could not be more evident than within the walls of the stadium today.  As Spence looks around at the wrestlers on the mats he can see something in their eyes that triggers his instinct about them.  He can sense the nerves and the fear that some posses just by the empty glare in their eyes, while others posses a focus, a concentration, a chill, and carry a strength that will undoubtedly help deliver them to the winner's podium. He recognizes in others, the eyes he wore a few years ago and he also recognizes those that share the eyes of confidence with him today. He peers across at the various "gateways to the soul" and locks in on a pair of focused and chilled eyes looking right back at him.

It's a quick glance with a subtle nod of the head. With Rudi's back toward Spence, Jake silently acknowledges his long time friend with a greeting fitting of a mere stranger and is then taken away by his coach. Spence watches as his East Temple rival walks back through the tunnel toward the locker rooms with Coach Rudi constantly jabbering in his ear.

After all the formalities of lining up in neat soldier-like rows, a few short speeches, and the National Anthem, the time finally arrives and the final state tournament for Spence, Jake and every other senior in the building begins. Nerves begin to rise to the surface and Jake hears a wrestler from another school throwing up in one of the stalls of the locker-room. Jake leaves to watch the action and waits for his first match. As he monitors the weight classes and calculates how long it will be until the 145 pounders will take the mat, he doesn't feel nerves he doesn't feel fear, he feels angry. Something inside him builds and he can feel it deep inside his gut. He pans his surroundings and the only thing he feels is himself getting mad. He's mad at the other wrestlers, the coaches, the officials and listening to the cheers from the stands, he becomes angry at the fans. It isn't something that he's experienced before but it's not something he is questioning. He just had it inside him right now and it's not going away.

Jake has music raging through his headphones and is pacing up and down the gym floor. It's just a few more moments before his final shot at a title begins but it seems like he's been waiting forever. The anger that filled him with energy has not only faded but has tired him. Now he feels the clammy sweat of his hands and the dryness of his throat confirming the magnitude of the moment. Nerves are starting to take over. Jake tries to get some adrenaline flowing by slapping his own face a few times. He continues to bounce and tries to gear up for his match and then he feels Rudi's hand pushing him and guiding him toward the mats.

"Okayeee let's go!"

Jake never heard his name announced and was surprised that he needed to be on the mat…right now! His routine was broken and suddenly he feels a rush of blood flow to his head. Strangely, it was just what he needed to get him back on track and served to wake him out of his trance. Walking onto the mat he can feel his body surge with strength. Looking out over the crowd and seeing his mother and all the fans in the stadium only serves to build his confidence. He's ready.

It doesn't take much time for Jake to earn the first takedown and go up 2-0. He partially releases his opponent but keeps his hands on the wrestlers head, pushing it down, showing dominance over the wrestler. When Tim Fields finally gets his one point for his "escape", he's greeted with blows to his head and shoulders as Jake pounds and pounds Fields to the edge of the mat, finally shoving him out of bounds. The score is only 2-1 but Jake has already won a mental war. Back at the center of the mat, the official warns Jake to keep working to score. This was a wrestling match, not a brawl and he wanted to make sure Jake didn't turn it into one.

Jake hardly acknowledges the referee and goes back to work and scores another takedown but doesn't allow fields to get back up this time. Jake throws in a leg and starts to work on Fields' arm. With a fast jerk, heeding no caution to Fields' safety, Jake yanks back Tim Fields arm and the referee immediately stops the action for Fields' protection. Jake is clearly pumped up and shakes his head in disapproval as he paces around the mat waiting to begin again.

It is then that he notices Spence two mats away putting the finishing touches on a match that would last just over 3 minutes. Spence has his man looking at the ceiling lights and is ready to move to the next round. When the action begins again, Jake feels a chance to take Fields to his back and in a move of panic and desperation Fields makes a mistake and finds himself with his back flat on the mat and in an instant, the match is over. Jake runs to the center of the mat and quickly removes his ankle bands with the haste of someone who is late for an appointment. After having his hand raised he runs off toward Spencer.

Spence is jogging off to find a place to run his sprints and feels the arm of his old friend wrap around his shoulders.

"Nice match!"

"Yeah, you too. Come by and see some of the guys later."

"Rudi doesn't like me hanging out with the *enemy.*"

Not knowing what to say to that, Spence just smiles, "Well, okay. I guess I'll see you in the finals."

As Spence jogs away he can't help to feel strange about how uncomfortable the 30 second conversation was. After a few sprints he takes a spot in the stands and takes some time to take it all in. He remembers some of the tournaments of the past. He recalls the many hours he spent in the stands in so many gyms across the state. He sees images of Jake, Coach, Tommy, Wes, Fontenetta, John Kim, and the rest of wrestling's extended family members. He looks down at one of the referees on the mats below and remembers the bad call he made in one of his matches a few years past. Spence closes his eyes as the nostalgic images continue and he puts back his head and rests, and remembers, and then realizes that these last few days might end up being the best of all his memories but it will also be the last.

Sarah Stevens tracks down the Jackson faithful and is greeted with hugs and smiles. It's always great to see old friends and enough time has past where the reunion can be had without too much sadness and tears. A warm comfort surrounds her with each hug and is like a blanket of calm that soothes all that pains her. The warmest of greetings is about to come.

"Now who is this young lady?"

"Oh Trey, so great to see you Hun. How is everyone dear?"

"Same as always, we're doing fine. Jake looks better than ever. Spence has his work cut out for him"

Sarah rolls her eyes and places a hand over her heart. "Oh, I don't know if I'll be able to watch that match. At least things will get back to normal when it's all over. Trey, I've never seen Jake like this before. He's so moody and angry. He's still adjusting. It's been hard. I hope when it's over he'll be able to put some things away and sort himself out, you know?"

"He'll be fine Sarah. You and Coach raised a great kid. I know he's proud right now. You know, I'm not sure if I'll be able to watch the match either." As a big smile spreads across Trey's face. "My heart's gonna be pounding more than either of them."

Spence's second match is with an old opponent, Chuck Ulis. Spencer was called for a slam and was DQ'd when Ulis could not continue. Chuck went on to win his next match but his shoulder was hurting so much that he couldn't go on any further. For Chuck, revenge for that match has been a source of motivation all season. For Spence, it's a match that took him out of the tournament, the tournament that marked the death of his coach, and was a match that he would like to soon forget. One look at Ulis as they step into the circle instantly reminds Spence of sitting in the Jackson gym and listening to the news and there is suddenly a lump in his throat as the whistle blows to wrestle.

Spence remembers the first match when Ulis took him down right off of the whistle and then started working on his shoulder. He couldn't let that happen again and Spence takes a stance that has one knee on the ground just to make sure he's low enough. Ulis stops his shot in mid-attack and they both come back up to their feet but as Ulis comes back up Spence goes to his attack and shoots to his legs. The takedown goes to Spence and this time he is the one who is putting in the legs and working on Ulis' shoulder. There was a time when Spence may have really made Ulis pay and his goal would be to inflict some pain to Chuck's shoulder. But that was in the past and Spence releases Ulis' arm to work another move and a few seconds later the referee is raising his hand for two back points. Soon the wind falls out of Chuck Ulis' sails as any thoughts of revenge have disappeared and Spencer's lead grows and time ticks away. The third period arrives and Ulis knows it's all but over. As Jake watches from a corner he sees his friend at the top of his game working methodically and smoothly. The time runs out and Spence moves on. .

After the match Spence quickly puts on some sweats and covers his head with his hood. He's done for the day and the six minutes he just put in will go a long way toward him making weight again tomorrow but he still wants to make sure he gets the most out of the sweat he has. Instead of doing his regular sprints, he bundles up and takes a seat in the stands to see what he'll be up against tomorrow night.

Jake runs out onto the mat and quickly straps on the green ankle bands that helps to identify one wrestler from the other for the referee. He stretches and moves impatiently as his opponent walks slowly onto the mat. The second match of the state tournament usually brings about a tough match but Jake is the recipient of a favorable draw. His opponent isn't particularly tough and won his last match by default when a wrestler didn't make weight. Like Spencer, Jake handles his second match with ease and Rudi is unusually calm in his chair. Late in the second period Jake is ahead by 8 points and can coast the rest of the way. From the side of the mat Rudi yells to "geeatt your work een", knowing that Jake will have to make weight tomorrow. Strategy like this can backfire if Jake was unexpectedly put on his back, but both Jake and Rudi are confident enough that this wouldn't happen, at least not in this match. Spence doesn't stay for the end of the match. There wasn't much to see and he has some running to still do.

Trying to keep his sweat going, Jake runs off the mat after having his hand raised and makes a bee-line right to the scales. Spence is already there in the locker room checking his weight.

"Hey, you had an easy one."

"Yeah. He wasn't too tough at all. How's your weight?"

"Three and a quarter. I wanna go home only one."

Spence meant he was 3.25 pounds over his weight and he wants to drop enough now to go home with only one more pound to lose. As he gets dressed to go run off his 2.25 pounds, Jake strips down hastily so he doesn't stop sweating while he checks his weight. A quick step on and off, a frantic effort to get dressed again and they are both off to sweat off s few pounds of water.

They both go off together like they have so many times in the past. Rudi sees them in the distance and can't help but to worry about Jake's intensity, but it's too late now. Their heads bob up and down in unison and Rudi can only watch. If he had his way, Jake would be running with another East Temple wrestler but Jake and Spence are out of reach now. Three more matches and Jake can be

Rudi's first state champ and his program will have taken an important step.

"Quarter finals, semi finals, and then the finals, 18 more minutes." Spencer's words are heard by his running partner but he's talking to himself as much as he is talking to Jake. They run through the long corridors of the stadium like robots, looking straight ahead and never breaking stride. As the sweat drips off each boy, so does the awkwardness and the wall that seemed to be between them recently. Conversations drift from mothers to girls, to movies and to camping trips. They plan to continue their trip and this time it'll just be the guys again; Spence, Tommy, Jake and his brother Jimmy. It made no sense to speak about tomorrow. It wasn't something either one wanted to discuss. They'd rather just let it happen.

Spencer looks down as his steps hit the carpet of the hallway and listens to Jake's words and he suddenly realizes the regret he feels in wrestling 145 this year. Could he have won the title at 152? If he went up a weight then maybe they both could have won a state title and shared in the glory together. As it is, his decision to stay down at 145 makes one of them a loser. If there's anyone to blame for this, it's him. He keeps his head down to the floor and suddenly the words spill out.

"Jake, I'm sorry."

Not knowing how to respond, Jake pretends for a moment that he doesn't know what Spence talking about. In the back of his mind he knows exactly what he's saying.

"Huh?"

"I should've gone 152. This sucks"

"Hey, you're stronger at 145 you don't know what you would've done at 52. But it will suck for you when you take second place." Jake doesn't even look at Spence but his smile is very clear to see.

That triggers an immediate smile on Spence and eases a small part of his mind for at least a little bit. The topic is avoided for the rest of the run as they both contemplate the results of tomorrow. The run continues for another twenty minutes spending time talking about the other wrestlers and the action they saw on day one. They talk about the bad calls and the lousy referee on mat four. They remember the overtime wins and the big upsets that always highlights a state tournament but in the back of their minds their thinking about tomorrow. The sweat is flowing and they race, stride for stride on their final lap.

"Ok, I'll see you later"

"Yeah, in about 12 minutes."

A handshake and a "dude-hug" later and they separate into opposite locker rooms. Tomorrow they face their last chance to become a champion and only one can succeed.


Spence and Trey Davis have "dinner" at the hotel tonight. Dinner for Spence consists of a tiny piece of steak, about five bites worth, and a small side salad. Trey just has a small bowl of soup and doesn't want to eat too much in front of his wrestler trying to make weight.

"Big day tomorrow eh?"

"I'm ready coach."

"That's what I'm here to tell you Spence. You ARE ready. You've never been more ready. Tomorrow you have a chance to be in the best position anyone can have. It might not seem like it, but you're going to remember that finals match forever. Assuming it's you and Jake, it'll be something that you'll both never forget. You just have to make sure you get to that last match!"

Spence listens intently but wishes Trey would stop for a moment so he can devour the tiny morsel of meat on his plate.

"I know, but I wish it didn't have to be against Jake."

"You're not listening son. Having it be with Jake makes it MORE special. There aren't any losers on the final mat of a state tournament, anyone that gets there is a champion and tomorrow you have a chance to share the same spotlight with Jake. How can it get any better?"

Trey pauses as if he was waiting for an answer but both know that there isn't any response that can be given to that question. Spence just looks into his coach's eyes and waits for more.

"Tomorrow night, when it's just you and Jake under the lights, the two best wrestlers in the state will be facing off and everyone in the stands will know it. You'll be exactly where you belong, both of you."

Spence stops chewing for a second and really hears Trey's words. He's been taught his final lesson of his high school career; and all that's left is to have it all play out.

Driving home with his mother and brother, Jake is quiet and stares out the window. Sarah is lost for words but feels a need to parent at this moment. She can feel her son's anxiety and she shares in the loss of his father. Searching for words to break the silence,

"I love you Hun."

Jake responds with a roll of his eyes and the required "I love you too mom."

Sarah returns. "No, listen to me. We're gonna be alright. We're gonna make it, together, the three of us. It's all going to be okay.

"I know mom." Jake's response is of the typical teenage dismissive tone that tells a parent to stop talking and leave me alone.

Now Sarah's tone changes and has more of a bite in her response. "Just listen. I miss your dad too! More than you even know. I miss him everyday and I still reach for him at night. There hasn't been a day when I didn't shed a tear for him. Not a single day."

Jake looks at her and reaches for her hand. Young James holds back some tears and closes his eyes for a moment to squeeze them back into his eyes.

"You boys need to know that the three of us are going to be alright and that your dad watches over us everyday. No matter what happens tomorrow or the next day, or in the days after that, we are going to be okay and we are going to be together."

She spoke with so much confidence that her words pierced through the hearts of the two boys. They both turned their heads and looked directly to their mother. As she finished her words and her emotions become too great, she pulled the car to the side of the road. She leans over to her sons and they embrace. They embrace not in sadness, but in love, and in effort to hold on to what they have. They embrace to cling onto each other. They embrace in recognition that they will weather the storms and overcome the obstacles, the three of them, together. Wrestling and tomorrow's finals had nothing to do with the conversation, yet it had everything to do with it. Jake realized that no matter what happens in the thirty foot circle tomorrow, the importance of his life is right next to him, within the confines of his mother's car sitting at the side of the road.

Some of this realization will fade and the anxiety of tomorrow will build again before the night is over, but there are times when words that embrace the heart take hold and never lose its grip.

After a "dinner" of a small morsel of pasta and salad, Jake goes to his room to lie down and stares at his ceiling. It's a past time he's acquired over the past week. With the last day of his seasons arriving tomorrow, Jake might spend much of the night staring at his ceiling. The eternity of the next several hours will leave a lot of time to think and allows the images and thoughts he's tried to keep in the shadows to come out and haunt him.

Jake can see himself standing with his hands raised in victory and in the same picture he sees Spence kneeling on the mat in defeat. Every so often his self-doubt creates images of getting pinned and looking up at the winner. He fights with his imagination most of the night until he drifts off into a restless slumber. Then, out of nowhere, the warm comfort of his mother's words blanket his doubts and smothers them into submission.

Unlike other recent days, when Jake and Spence saw each other, on finals morning they quickly greet each other and wish a "good luck" as they move along to the tasks of the rest of the day. They each have to win two more matches before reaching the finals tonight. They quickly go their separate ways and back to their normal rituals. After weigh-in they prepare for the next match. The matches go by one after another and the noise in the stadium is filled with the hum of the crowd and the regular shrieks of referee whistles. Tim Decker, the reporter that did the story on Jake and Spence is on hand to watch how his story will resolve. He looks at the mass of wrestlers in the warm up area. He scans the sea of athletes and finally recognizes Spence at one edge of the mat stretching and massaging his thigh.

"You're not hurt are you?"

"Hey, Mr. Decker! Of course not. Just tryin to get some of the kinks out!"

"Do you have a few seconds for a quick interview?"

"If you can ask while I'm getting warmed up."

"Sure no problem. What did you think about your matches yesterday?"

"I'm feeling pretty good. No injuries, no weight issues. I wrestled pretty well yesterday but it'll have to be better today."

"Did you see any of Jake's matches?"

A big smile spreads across Spencer's face and he just shrugs his shoulders.

"A little, but I've seen him wrestle lots of times before. Ya know? Make sure you get a good seat. It's gonna be a good one." And then an even bigger smile shines across his face. Spence shows a confidence and an ease that rivals Tom Chernich. As Spence shakes Decker's hand and jogs away he thinks the same thing. That he sounds like Tommy.

Jake doesn't see Decker coming his way as he drills with an East Temple team mate. Decker waits patiently as the two boys drill over and over until Jake finally notices the reporter in the corner of his eye.

"Hey! I didn't see you there."

"I can see you're busy. Can I talk to you after your next match?"

"Sure anytime. My first match will be coming up soon. Where will you be?"

"Okay, don't worry, I'll find you. Good luck."

Jake simply nods and smiles. He feels sharp and right now he's never been so confidant that he's going to be a state champ. As he turns to drill with his partner, Decker jots into his book and hopes that neither of the boys disappoint. His article has placed an even brighter spotlight onto Spence and Jake, and the wrestling community is hoping to see the two of them play out what Decker has put into prose.

Jake and Spence are wrestling their opponents on mats 7 and 8. Both matches are right next to each other and at the same time. Watching the two of them prepare side by side, it becomes clear they arrive to the mat with the same history, the same training, the same pedigree. There movements are similar as they both sprint out to the center to put on the colored ankle bands, the quickly turn their backs to the outside of the circle not giving their opponent the courtesy of a glance. Spence takes a moment to break his concentration to walk over Jake's mat and give him a quick hand shake and a wish of luck. Jake smiles, shakes his friend's hand and looks up in the stands to see both his mother and Mrs. Howard looking down on their sons.

When the action starts Jake and Spence are right on top of their opponents. High speed perfection is the best way to describe the ease of their takedowns. Like Batman and Robin beating up the bad guys, Jake and Spence work side by side and dismantle their challengers.

Spencer has his match well in hand and Jim Alvarez has to come up with a miracle in the last period to stay in the hunt. Jim looks over to the score and sees a 6 point deficit. His coach calls to him and simply says, "You need a big move!"

With a minute remaining in the match and both wrestlers on their feet, Alvarez has nothing to lose and tries for a "big move". Alvarez grabs one of Spencer's arms and tries to whip Spence over his hip. Alvarez catches Spence off-guard for a split second but Spence recovers and pulls his arm away from a tight twisting grip that might have cost him a large lead. Spence moves around and finishes the match with another two points. Trey Davis breathes easy and so does Janice Howard, but hidden in the stoic calm of Spencer Howard's face, there is concern. As his hand is raised by the referee, he conceals the feeling of sharp daggers piercing his shoulder. He grits his teeth and to those watching, everything seems to be par for the course. Underneath, Spence is in pain and the energy and confidence he felt all week begins to drain away. Trey can sense something is wrong. Spence walks off the mat without starting his customary sprints, his face is white and without expression, and there is a definite worry in his eyes.

"It's my shoulder."

"Okay, I'll have someone get some ice. Let's go to the locker room so you can show me how much motion you have."

They hustle to the farthest locker room to try and find some privacy. If the shoulder is real bad, having his next adversary learn about it in advance wouldn't help matters any. Going right to the trainer is out. If it is serious, there is a chance the trainer might try and force Spence to not wrestle. This wasn't going to be an option so it's ice and an initial evaluation by Coach Trey.

"Okay Spence, show me how much you have without any pain at all."

Spence winces and slowly moves his left arm forward and around in a very small and unsteady circle. With his eyes closed, Spence moves it around a few more times to see if he can get any more flexibility from his arm.

"Alright." Trying to hide his concern, Trey reaches out and takes hold of Spencer's left arm and gives it some needed support. "Try to give it as much motion as you can, bearing as much pain as you can."

Spence takes a deep breath and squeezes his eyes as he lifts his shoulder and winds it around, rotating his shoulder to about 80% of what the normal amount of motion should be.

"That's not bad but it's gonna get stiffer and harder to move as the day goes on. Let's see the trainer now while you have this amount of movement in it and then we'll ice."

They quickly walk to the trainer's room. Trey pulls out some ibuprofen out of his small medicine kit as they pass by a water fountain.

"Take a couple of these for the inflammation"

They both walk with purpose and nothing more is said. Their concerns shout loud and clear in their silence.

Jake's match ends in a 6-4 nail biter as a takedown in the final minute sealed his victory. Rudi tells Jake that he better "wake up" for the next match. Jake knows just what he means. He knows it wasn't his best wrestling but it's not the first time his first match of the day was uninspiring. His last takedown was smooth as silk and he rode the rest of the period out without any problems.

"Don't worry coach; I'm just hitting my stride. I just needed that warm up this morning."

Mike Fontenetta, who's next win will put him in the 140 finals, passes by Jake and shakes his hand. Nothing is really said, just a handshake and a nod is enough for the two of them. Small talk and words of congratulations seems a little empty at this point in the tournament. Every wrestler is either too focused or too nervous to waste time on too many pleasantries. Jake jogs past to find a place to do his ritual sprints. The season ends today so at this point, he does it more out of superstition than preparation. As he runs, he wonders for a moment why he hasn't spotted Spence doing his customary sprints as well but the thought passes quickly.

He is one more win away from his finals match with Spence. He runs and thinks of his father. Jake sees the casket and the endless rows of flowers that lined the room. He remembers the times when Coach hugged him and the few times when he yelled. Jake thinks about the camping trips and dinners as a family and also dinner as the extended family with Coach Trey, Spence and his mom. He runs hard and never tires. A strength fills his muscles as he remembers. It's been about a month since he last cried about his father and thinking about him now makes him sad but in a different way. The memories fill Jake instead of drain him. He can almost hear his dad telling him to focus on his next match. He feels strong and comforted and after his last sprint he pauses for a moment so that he can come back to this feeling again, like placing a bookmark in time so he can re-read a favorite passage.

Spencer finds himself a quiet place in the stadium stands and hopes to not be noticed. His warm-up jacket covers the pack of ice wrapped around his shoulder. Spot lights cast brilliance over the mats below and he sits in shadows that hide his worry while his maturity hides his fear. He sits alone and gazes out onto the floor saying nothing and trying his best to think of nothing as well. His shoulder begins to numb under the cold of the ice. The ache in his shoulder is calm for the moment but he knows that too much movement of his arm will cause a spasm of pain.

Coach Davis tells him to just keep the shoulder quiet for a while. He wants Spence to calm down and hopefully his shoulder can relax a little too. It won't be too long before he has to step onto the mat again and his shoulder will need to be ready. After about twenty minutes of ice, Spence carefully moves his arm. His face contorts into several ugly grimaces but he can move his arm around just about a full large circle. Spence says it feels better and starts to put on some ointment to warm up the shoulder. Trey smiles with some gratification but he knows that the real test will come later on.

The semi-finals have begun and senior, Mike Fontenettta, warms up in the corner with Spencer. Mike didn't have a chance to come here last year after losing his wrestle off to Wes Carlson, but today he has his chance. One more win and he steps onto the mats tonight under the bright spotlight, in front of thousands of wrestlers and fans. If he loses he drops down to battle back for a third place and fight off a possible drop down to a 6th place finish. Usually the two of them would be sparring with each other, but Spencer's shoulder won't allow it. Spence paces around in circles rotating his arm to get as much movement as he can and to test the limits of his shoulder. Fontenetta warms up with Assistant Coach Carlson and is geared up to get started. The PA system announces the 140 pound wrestlers to report to the mats. Spence looks to Mike and gives him a hug and a handshake. "Go get it Mike!"

Fontenetta runs off. Before Trey follows behind he looks over his shoulder to Spence and tells him to "stay warm and keep moving it."

Spence keeps moving and bouncing and tries to look in between and over other coaches and wrestlers in the entrance hall, trying to get a glimpse of Fontenetta's match. Jake arrives to the warm up area with Coach Rudi and they drill with some hand fighting. The warm up area is thick with tension as some wrestlers try to hide the times when they sneak peaks at their opponents, others stare them down without apology, and still others are poised and focused enough to zone out most everything around them. Spence can only think about his shoulder and getting it loose. Jake works with Rudi and he is focused on nothing else. None of them feel the eyes that glare at them all during their warm-ups.

Sal Genovese, the wrestler ranked third in the weight class, watches Jake intently. Genovese is a transfer student and a former Illinois State Champion. Genovese has the look of a wrestler, complete with a neck wider than his head, forearms that seem larger than his biceps and with cauliflower ears that are puffed and swollen from the affects of many years in the sport. Because of the timing of his transfer, Sal had to sit out almost the entire first half of the season. His record is perfect yet all season long he's had to suffer through hearing about the two favorites, Spencer and Jake. There is nothing he'd like better than to be the spoiler and knock out Jake in the tournament.

About twenty feet away, Clarence Golden prepares to wrestle Spencer. He lost to Wes Carlson last year in the Regionals and has struggled to make the 145 pound weight class all season. He looks like a body builder and his lack of body fat displays his muscularity like a medical anatomy book.

Suddenly a roar has the waiting group of wrestlers stop and look out toward the mats. It's the Jackson High crowd that has erupted to Mike's come from behind pin that will take him to the finals match tonight. Mike jumps into Wes Carlson's arms and is lifted off his feet. Wes wipes the tear from his eye and fights the choking feeling in his throat. Along with the joy of having his old team mate and friend succeed, there is an ease to the guilt he has carried for taking Fontenetta out of competition last year. Mike runs off the floor, swept up in his own celebration. On the way out, he is congratulated by Spence and then by Jake. Mike Fontenetta is six minutes away from becoming a state champion.

Rudi pulls on Jake's arm and tells him to get focused and block out everything around him. Jake seems to snap back into a mode of intensity and stares into Rudi's eyes. Rudi peers back and looks for signs that his wrestler is in the right frame of mind.

When the 145 pound wrestlers are announced, Rudi glances over to Spencer and sees a reaction of pain on his face. He watches closely and looks for more signs of injury but Spence hides his discomfort well enough for the time being. Spence and Jake jog to the mats ahead of the rest of other wrestlers and coaches. As they split, Jake looks over with a smile

"See you in about 6 minutes."

They touch fists and go to their respective mats. Clarence Golden walks to the center of the mat and stares down Spence, who could not be more unaware of his opponent.

"How's it feel?"

"No problem coach. I'm good."

Trey knows that Spence is saying only what he wants to believe and what his coach wants to hear. The truth is that he's doing his best to ignore the pain and work past it. It's time to tough it out.

"Keep pushing him. He's going to tire out in the third."

The only problem is that the last thing Spence wants is to have to go a whole 6 minutes. He wants to finish as soon as possible to protect his shoulder. He wants to limit the pain he will have to face with every minute of the match. The sooner it's over, the better.

Some wrestlers are intimidated by the physical appearance of Clarence Golden, but Spencer can't be bothered by any of that. He looks Golden right in the eyes and puts out his hand and is ready to roll. The whistle blows and Spence goes right to work. He pushes and pulls, and attempts to set up his shot. Spence shoots a double leg and Golden sprawls his legs back and leans on Spencer's left shoulder. The pain makes Spence release the leg and his eyes close in agony. Golden works to get the takedown and Spencer finally gives up the two points. The action moves across the mat and goes out of bounds. As the two go back to the center, Coach Davis calls to Spence.

"Set up a single leg!"

This meant to go after a single leg takedown that way pressure can stay off of Spencer's shoulder when going for a shot. First, Spence needs to get away from Golden before he can think about taking him down. Golden slips in a leg and Spence slams his hip to the mat and works on freeing himself from Golden's laced leg. Golden, working legs is a lucky break for Spence. Golden's strength going after Spence's arms would put a huge strain on the injured shoulder. Spence works on getting Golden out of position. He lifts Golden's leg and turns toward his hips. Spence snakes his arm through and wraps around Golden's waist, two reversal.

The second period begins with Spence choosing the defensive position and scores a quick escape to take a 3-2 lead. Spence keeps up his attack and in the process learns what his shoulder will and will not allow. Near the end of the period Spence knows the limitations of his arm and begins to move with confidence. In his head, he goes through his vast knowledge of wrestling and identifies what will hurt and not hurt his shoulder. He sifts through the files of maneuvers like a computer program. Spence works fast and surprises Golden. He reaches across with his right hand and trips Golden at his knee for another takedown.

With the score 5-2 Spencer feels the throb in his

shoulder growing. Golden scrambles and turns hard and tries to hit a switch to reverse positions. The pressure on his shoulder is too much and Spence pushes Golden away and gives up an escape and a point making the score 5-3. The second period ends and the "cat jumps out of the bag" as Spence is clearly in pain. His arm sags down and seems to pull the rest of his body down toward the floor. There's no hiding the injury now. Spence reaches for his shoulder as if to keep his arm from falling off onto the mat. Coach Davis asks for an injury time-out and Spence winces his way to the corner of the mat. Coach Carlson hands Spence a water bottle as Trey Davis holds Spence's arm at the elbow to relieve some of the pressure on his shoulder. As the weight of his arm is lifted by Coach Davis, Spencer exhales a sigh of relief. Janice Howard stands to her feet and covers her face, peeking through her fingers to watch what she cannot bear to view.

It takes about a minute of injury time for the pain to ease and Spence to be ready to wrestle. Clarence Golden now has a clear target of attack, but like Trey Davis anticipated, Golden is beginning to have struggles of his own. Golden wrestled up at 152 all season long. Dropping down to 145 for two straight days is taking its toll. As Spencer was taking his injury time, Clarence Golden was using the time to catch his breath and recover. After wrestling ended yesterday, Golden spent the next hour sweating down. He dehydrated himself and fasted in order to make weight today. Right now his hands and legs are tingling. He's having a hard time catching his breath and the massive physique is far weaker than it appears to be.

The third period begins with both wrestlers are struggling to perform to his capabilities. Spence is ahead by two and he makes half-hearted attempts at Golden's legs. The strategy of survival has begun and Spence is trying to hang on and protect his shoulder. Clarence Golden needs a takedown to tie but his body screams for oxygen and the energy to continue. Spence sees his opponent's slow reaction time and keeps moving. Conditioning may be the difference that wins this battle. Clarence Golden makes his own half-hearted attempts to attack, hoping for Spencer to make some kind of mistake and leave himself open. When Golden makes another attempt, Spencer counters and gets a strong grip on Golden's left leg. Spencer finishes the takedown easily with Golden out of gas and just running on fumes. Spence is up by 4 points now, and gives up an escape with 30 seconds to go. Spence stays away and gives up a stalling point as time runs out. When the referee takes his left arm to raise it in victory, Spence pulls it away and gives him his right arm instead. He'll have about 5 hours before his final match. It's time to get another bag of ice and heal as much as he can.


Rudi's eyes float back and forth from his mat to Spencer's. He can see how the Jackson star is hurting and knows Jake will be in great shape for a championship if he can get past Sal Genovese. Earlier, Rudi was worried about Jake's intensity, but Jake needs no extra motivation for this match. Thanks to Coach Rudi, he knows all about Genovese. He's watched video of Sal and read about his accomplishments as last year's Illinois State Champion.

"Hee ees a tough wrestler. Maybee beatter than Spencer even."

Rudi has made certain that both he and Jake are prepared for this one. Aside from the fact that it's the semi-finals of the state tournament, the fact that he's wrestling a State Champ has Jake geared up and wired tight. Jake is full of energy before the match begins and there's a definite bounce in his steps as he paces around the large circle of the mat. He bobs his head up and down, and then he looks to the ceiling and seems to be talking to himself as if he was trying to calm himself down. Jake moves his hands, almost like a boxer, as he plays out moves in his head. The referee calls them to the center and they begin.

Immediately Sal attacks and hammers Jake on the back of his head with a right hand. Sal drives his forehead into Jake's temple and Jake feels like his head is being squeezed in a vice. Genovese is more physical than anyone Jake has faced this season. Rudi watches with some admiration to his style, the style he is trying to install to the East Temple team. For Jake, wrestling Genovese isn't much different from wrestling Coach Rudi; hard nosed, in your face, aggressive, boarder line over the top. Jake matches the aggression with his own and the battle begins to become a war. They pound, push and attack with a relentless violence that makes the fans in the stands take notice. Neither is willing to back down an inch and as the action moves to the edge of the mat, Sal gives Jake a shove off the mat. Jake takes a step to Genovese to respond in kind, but the referee steps in between the boys.

Rudi claps loudly and gives Jake a confirming nod and a look of appreciation for the work he's showing on the mat. The message is to just keep it up, stay tough. The action begins again just as it was: banging, pounding, hammering back and forth. There is little finesse to this match, just brutal force and undying will. Jake hammers back and forth with Genovese and then, purely out of instinct, he ducks around Sal's frontal assault and scores a slick takedown that triggers a collective "Ooooohhhhh" from the crowd.

Rudi jumps three feet into the air and claps even more loudly. The sweat begins to show on the back of Rudi's shirt and his enthusiasm adds to the drama of the match. There are 5 other matches in progress but all eyes are on Jake and Sal. Genovese works to get to his feet but Jake works him back down to the mat. Jake makes an effort to turn Sal but ends up in a scramble and suddenly finds himself in a bad position. Genovese takes control and reverses Jake for 2 points and ties the score. As the end of the first period approaches, Jake gets to his feet but cannot break away from Genovese's grip and the clocks hits triple zeros. Jake looks over to Rudi looking for some help, he knows he's in a dog fight. 2-2

The second period starts with both wrestlers on their feet again. Jake takes a fast shot and gets in deep on a leg but Sal counters by wrapping his arms around Jakes waist and sitting his hip to the mat. Jake works to get some control as the two wrestlers twist and turn to seek some sort of advantage. Jake holds onto Sal's legs and pops underneath. Sal ends up over and behind Jake's back, upside down and grabbing hold of Jake's ankles. Jake turns back toward his opponent and secures one leg while Sal also hangs on to one of Jake's legs. They jostle back and forth and just as it looks as if one will gain control the other takes the opportunity away. Jake takes Sal's leg and rolls madly around to his stomach and he finds himself with just enough leverage to earn a takedown. The flurry brings about a cheer from the crowd in appreciation of the performance. 4-2, Jake.

Genovese works up to his feet again but Jake can't hang on to him and Jake finds himself hanging on to a 4-3 lead. The action heats up again as they go back to hammering each other. They bash back and forth and as they brawl themselves off the mat, both wrestlers give a shove and for a split second each thinks about taking a swing at the other. The referee steps in and calls from the stands yell for the official to give penalty points.

There are times in the sport of wrestling when there is a lack of action and athletes are too cautious. Officials need to prod the combatants to attack and warn them for inaction. Rules are in place to help assure that wrestlers continue to wrestle and engage their opponent. None of that is required in this match. The energy in the match seems to build for both Jake and Sal and they become more active as the match continues. It's as if the excitement of the action is feeding them both with

193

adrenaline.

The crowd reactions and the excitement in the air draws Spence back to the mat area. An ice pack creates a conspicuous bulge under his warm-up jacket as he finds a good spot to enjoy the show with all the other wrestling fans.

The wrestling begins again and the two are locked together with their arms hooked and intertwined. Sal takes a deep step and fakes reaching for Jakes leg. When Jake reacts, Sal Genovese executes the move of the day by sweeping Jake's other leg out from under him. Jake topples over like a house of cards and Jake finds himself behind 5-4.

For those in the front row of the stands, Spencer Howard's voice can be heard clearly.

"Let's go Jake!"

For the start of the final period, Jake takes the defensive position planning to get a quick escape and tie the match. Genovese throws in his legs by lacing his leg around Jake's. Sal thinks that he can ride him better by using his legs, but as soon as Sal's leg laces through, Jake raises his hips and does a forward roll and ends up on top.

"TWO!! TWO!!" Rudi's screams pierce the stadium from the corner of the mat but just as the second "TWO" is called out Sal adjusts and takes control back from Jake. The referee merely shakes his head, communicating that there are no points awarded. With that frenzy of action many in the crowd have come to their feet to watch what has become the best match of the day. Jake keeps working and nearing the end of the period there are signs that the two wrestlers are trying to catch their breath from the frenzied pace. Jake takes a look at the clock and knows that he has to get his escape point. Rudi yells from the side.

"You mahst score!! Get one! Get one!"

Jake takes another look at the clock and sees time ticking away and he becomes frantic to get away. He works his way up to his feet but Sal still has a hold of him. Sal brings Jake back down to the mat and at the same time is able to turn Jake's back to the mat for just a quick second. The referee, however, thought it was a bit longer than a single second and awards Sal Genovese two big back points to give Sal a 7-4 lead.

Now Rudi is beside himself and screams his disbelief.

"What een the world are you lookeeng at??"

The official ignores the coach and keeps his eyes on the wrestlers. Jake knows the situation and gathers himself enough to scoot his hips underneath him and he kicks out his legs to "hip heist" his way out of Sal's grasp to escape and make the score 7-5. Jake is running out of time and goes right to work and is able to grab one of Sal's arms with two hands in what is called "Russian tie". Genovese pushes Jake's head away and it's just what Jake is hoping for. With his left hand, Jake reaches over his head to grab Sal's arm. With a quick yank Jake is able to spin Sal around and suddenly Sal Genovese's legs are completely exposed and Jake gets the takedown.

The stadium erupts as the score is now tied and fans throughout the arena look to each other and predict "overtime". Several fans look to each other and ask

"What was that?"

"Did you see that?"

"What was that move?"

The truth is that there isn't a name for it. Jake put it together himself and he hasn't seen anyone else do it before.

Jake and Sal are showing signs that the frantic pace of this match is wearing them both down. As the referee walks to the table to double check that the score is correct, both Jake and Sal stand with their hands on their hips, just looking at each other as if they can't believe the battle they are in the midst of. Sweat drips down from their faces and their chests pump with each breath.

Overtime is one minute long. The victory goes to the first wrestler to score a point. The period begins with both wrestlers afraid to make a mistake that will cost him the match. The aggressive action that filled the first 6 minutes of the match has disappeared and Jake and Sal go to a mode of sparring back and forth with caution. A bad shot or a careless stance and the match can be over in an instant. The referee tries to get them going with some encouragement.

"Don't stop wrestling now guys."

Jake and Sal hear but don't listen. Neither wants to make the mistake that costs them the match. Then Jake gets impatient and takes a shot but Sal is ready. He sprawls back and ends up having Jakes head and arm in a front headlock. Jake immediately works to drag out of the position and Sal works to get behind Jake. Jake pulls hard and is almost around to Genovese's back but Sal turns hard and faces Jake. They end up both back on their feet with no point change. Genovese takes a quick shot hoping to catch Jake off-guard, but Jake is always ready to protect his legs after a flurry. He fights off the attack and the overtime period ends with no change.

The marathon match goes to the next stage. Two tiebreaker periods of 30 second each. Entering the eighth minute of the match Sal takes the bottom position. Both wrestlers are struggling for oxygen and their muscles are screaming for rest. Jake takes his position and Sal intentionally jumps the whistle for a false start. This gives him a few more seconds of rest and a few more breaths of oxygen that might feed into his fatigued muscles. Jake sees Sal looking exhausted but he actually has more energy than he lets on. On the next whistle, Sal explodes and catches Jake off-guard with a stand up and gets an immediate escape. Jake has to get after him right away and immediately goes after a leg. He's able to pull one of Sal's legs into the air and struggles to finish but finally gets his points before the 30 seconds end.

Jake is ahead by a point going into the final 30 seconds. For the first time in the match Jake is in the driver's seat. He is just 30 seconds away from victory. Jake has the bottom position and off the whistle Sal lets Jake go and hopes for a takedown to tie the score again. Thirty seconds isn't a lot of time to finish a takedown. Jake stays low and defends. The clock ticks down and Sal Genovese knows the end is near. He takes a shot in desperation and Jake flattens him out to the mat. The match ends. Jake slowly stands and walks to the center of the mat. Sal remains on the mat with his head buried in his hands. The official moves to Genovese and bends down to be heard.

"Let's go young man. That was a great match."

Jake and Sal briefly embrace and the crowd stands in applause. Jake escapes a close call and Sal Genovese must begin his battle for a third place finish. Coach Rudi is ecstatic and so is Jake but he doesn't have the energy to express any of his joy. His next match is later tonight but all he wants to do now is lie down and catch his breath. Tonight, the stands will be full, emotions will be high, and the outcomes will last for an eternity.

# Final Match

Spencer goes back to the hotel to rest and wait for the evening session of the finals matches. The break gives him time to nap, time for his aching shoulder to rest, time to have a meal, and also time to think. He digs into his suitcase and pulls out "The Letter". It is his most prized possession from his dad. It is a letter written for Spence right after a youth wrestling match. Matt Howard was waiting for Spencer to get a bit older before giving him the letter but he never had the chance. A few days after Matt Howard's last days, Janice found the letter in Matt's desk drawer. It took Janice two years before she was ready to present Spence with his father's final message. Spence reads it from time to time but hasn't had the strength to read it again since Coach Stevens' accident.

*Spence,*

*You had a tough time on the mat today and the ride home was pretty quiet. I admit I was very disappointed but I later came to realize that I shouldn't be and that it is all part of the journey you are taking.*

*When I watch you on the mat I worry that you are doing battle while unprepared and that I have failed in your preparation. As a father that is my greatest fear, that you are unprepared to face the challenges that will come before you. I want you to be prepared for your match, but I've come to realize that it is the matches themselves that, are in the long run, win or lose, the things that ARE preparing you.*

*I think that the greatest benefit from wrestling is learning to face challenges and to demand the most from yourself. You learn to fight when you think there is no more fight left within you. You learn to get up after you've fallen, time and time again. You learn about sacrifice and about pain.*

*You learn to endure and to overcome. This is what I want for you, not because I wrestled, but because these lessons are the true gifts of this sport. So, those losses today were actually part of this gift, and an important part of the journey.*

*My dream for you is to not just win championships and fill your room with medals. My dream for you is much greater and I hope you get much more from wrestling. I hope you learn to strive for greatness even if you fail in the attempt. I hope you learn to get up one more time when you think you can't get up any longer. I hope you learn to not only face your fears, but to stare them down.*

*Wrestling isn't about winning. It is about the desire to win. It isn't about success, but rather the determination to succeed. I want you to succeed as a wrestler, not to win state championships, but I want you to be a successful wrestler so you learn to be all that you can. This sport can help teach you that, if you let it. I look forward to the seasons of our future as you go through these lessons and I'll be in your corner for each and every one of them.*

*I love you.*

*Dad*

Spence still can't read the letter without feeling his eyes begin to swell and Janice Howard keeps a framed copy of it in her bedroom. Today, Spence reads the letter in the quiet of his hotel room, just a few short hours to the last match of his High School career. He wonders if somewhere in the stadium, somewhere unseen at the corner of the mat, will his father be there watching over him? Will Coach Stevens be at his side?

With Rudi as his coach, Jake has less quiet time to himself and after his exhausting semi-finals match he wants to make sure he has some time to close his eyes. Rudi and Jake sit together in an isolated part of the stands to talk over the last match. Rudi sings his same song about being aggressive and being physical for all six minutes. He reminds Jake that he is one match away from a state title he should already have, as if he needed any reminders.

"Reemember Jaeeke, you are stronger theean Spence. Teaake adveantage of that."

Jake can only nod his head. Rudi has become hard to listen to but at the same time Jake thinks that he might not have been able to get past Sal Genovese if it wasn't for the training he has gone through with Rudi. Jake was able to beat the physical style of Genovese. Last season he might not have been able to do that. All season long he's been able to combine all the lessons he's learned from his father with some new lessons from his new coach, and he's been successful. Jake just wonders if it will be enough for tonight.

At precisely 6 p.m. the wrestlers begin their march through the tunnel into the stadium floor. The lights are out and athletes and coaches are guided by spotlights dancing throughout the building. At the end of the procession Jake and Spence find themselves across from one another at opposite ends of the mat. There is no greeting and little acknowledgement at all, other than a nod of the head. They both stare at the flag and step from side to side as the National Anthem plays. Each wrestler stands quiet and reflective, anticipating the moments about to come.

After the anthem, a booming voice from the PA system thunders though the building. As each wrestler is announced they jog to the center of the mat to shake hands with their opponent. Spence and Fontenetta stand together as 140 and 145 pound representatives. Mike looks around at the masses of people filling the stands soaking in all of the pageantry. Spence does his best to keep his head down and just listen for his name.

"At 140 pounds Michael Fontenetta from Jackson High School, Coached by Trey Davis"

The crowd comes to their feet at the mention of

Jackson High with an explosion of applause. Mike understands that the show of appreciation isn't only for him, but it's for the team and for Coach Stevens. Mike looks around at the crowd and returns the applause by raising his hands high toward the crowd and clapping them together in thanks. As Fontenetta returns to his place next to Spence he puts his head down and doesn't say another word.

Jake and Spence will be announced next and they each try to summon up the emotional strength to face the greeting that is about to come. The crowd doesn't wait to begin their ovation and neither wrestlers can hear the announcement of their names so both Jake and Spence walk to the center at the same moment. At the center of the mat they lock in an embrace that is clearly more than that of congratulations but also of remembrances, appreciation, gratitude, consoling and friendship. As Spence walks back to his end of the mat, Jake doesn't return to his opposing side. Instead he runs past Spence and heads toward Mike Fontenetta and Coach Trey and gives them each an embrace. As Jake releases Coach Trey he shakes his hand and controls the emotions that try to quiver his words, "Thanks for everything Coach."

Trey smiles and pats his former wrestler on the back.

"It's going to be a great match. Good luck."

Jake runs back to his end of the mat and Rudi has nothing to say but gives Jake a disapproving look. Whether Rudi's anger was because he felt betrayed by Jake or just because he wants Jake to stay focused is something that only he will ever know. Nothing is said and Jake has no reaction or response to Rudi's glare.

After the ceremony concludes, the 103 pound wrestlers get started, 112 and 119 pound wrestlers continue to stay warm and the rest of the athletes have to wait. The adrenaline of the opening ceremony can be intoxicating. There's a pageantry that can take a young man's breath away. The ceremony can seem so grand that the actual match can be a let down. When it's over and you have to sit and wait, the heart slows, the body cools, and for some, fatigue begins to takeover the body. For Jake and Spence the ceremony is just another formality.

In a corner of the stadium, Coach Davis applies some ointment to Spencer's shoulder. He's been desperately trying to get as much motion as possible and the heat applied to the shoulder helps just a little bit more.

"I'll be okay coach!"

"I know you will. Just keep moving it and you'll be fine."

They each wonder how much the other is lying. There isn't much else to do but to be positive.

Jake sits alone in a locker room, his knees bent up to his chest and his hood covering his head. In his mind he runs through his final match, his eyes closed and his thoughts racing. Coach Rudi walks in on his wrestler but then walks right back out of the locker room. Rudi has plenty to say but gives his wrestler a few more moments alone. Jake sits quietly, bundled up to stay warm and loose. His focus shuts out anything around him and he submerges himself in his trance. His thoughts are about nothing except the match. There are no images of failure, no thoughts of his father, of Jackson, or his friendship with Spencer. In the distance he can hear the muffled sounds of matches beginning and ending. The reactions of the crowd have a rhythm to it and give evidence to the ending of each match. Jake just sits, listens and waits for his time.

"Ok Jake leeatts get out theeere."

With that, Jake runs out with Rudi following right behind. They move to the warm-up area and it's as if a switch has been pulled and Jake is turned himself on to another gear. He bounces in that familiar fashion common among wrestlers, back and forth on the balls of his feet. He looks straight ahead to the mats with Coach Rudinoff right in his ear.

"Right now Jake, your beeast 6 meenutes right now! Thees ees your last chance and you'll naver get thees moment back again. Eeentensity."

Jake nods in agreement and then he hears his name called over the speakers.

The moment has come and the Jackson fandom comes to their feet. After just witnessing Mike Fontenetta lose a heartbreaking match to take a second place, they're energy is again recharged. Neither wrestler looks up and Spence continues to move his shoulder, convincing himself that it's much better than it really is. All eyes fall on their mat as many in the stands have been awaiting this very match. Tim Decker prepares to finish his story and quickly jots down more notes into his pad and sits just a few feet away from the action. Coach Davis takes Spence by the shoulders and looks him straight in the eyes. He speaks with a fatherly, calm tone but one that delivers an unmistakable confidence.

"Go do it young man. It's right out there for you. You just have to go get."

When Spence and Jake run out to the center of the mat there are no greetings and no smiles. For each, it's their last chance and the moment that they've been awaiting, and dreading, is right now. Their handshake is a mere slap of the palms like they have done hundreds of times before. The official brings his head down to say a few words.

"Here we go guys. I don't think I have to remind you to keep wrestling. Good luck to you both." He steps away and blows the whistle.

Jake comes in as expected and starts to bang away, trying to be more physical and take Spence out of his game. He pounds on Spencer's head but Spence locks up his arms to stop some of the punishment and try to get some control. The two go back and forth but without either one making any real attempt at a takedown. Even though they haven't wrestled each other in over a year, they begin to recall some of the old habits of the other and also realize some differences as well.

Spence is amazed at how strong Jake feels while Jake can't seem to get a hold of Spence like he used to. Spence seems to anticipate and Jake can't seem to get to his offense. Jake takes a shot and backs off and immediately attacks again with a "duck under". Spence counters and faces off and the two begin to scramble for an advantage. The flurry leads them to the edge of the mat and finally they roll out of the circle. The whistle blows but neither wrestler seems to hear, or cares to listen to it. Just like they used to do in the Jackson wrestling room, they keep wrestling as they go off the mat and onto the rubber floor of the stadium. The two of them break on their own and race back to the circle. The referee warns both of them about stopping at the whistle but both boys only stare across at one another, neither one was going to stop until the other did.

Spence has had enough of Jake pounding on his head and manages to lock up one of Jakes arms in a "Russian Tie". Spence uses both his hands and grips Jakes arm tight to his chest. Jake pushes Spence's head away and tries to get his arm back. He reaches to pull Spence's elbow to loosen his grip but then feels an opportunity. In that split second, thought turns to action and Jake underhooks one arm and ducks under the other and gets the first points of the match.    Spence shakes his head, mad at himself for the mistake. Jake gets the first two points but can't hold down Spence. Spence immediately comes to his feet and cuts away from Jake.  (2-1 Jake)

Jake goes right back to his game plan and starts to attack at Spencer's head. Spence shoots low and dives for an ankle. Jake tries to counter but Spence has his takedown now and is beginning to wrap his leg around Jake's.  (3-2 Spence) Spence tries to work for a turn but Jake is just too strong. Spencer is riding Jake pretty well but Jake elevates his hips and rolls over his shoulder, trying to loosen Spencer off of him. Once again, the wrestling moves to the edge of the mat and just as they move out of the circle Jake is able to free his leg and get an escape as they move out of bounds. The first period ends with the score tied at 3.

The second period begins and the flip of a referee's coin wins Spencer the choice of position and elects to both be on their feet. Spence breaths a quiet sigh of relief. His fear was that Jake might know how bad the shoulder was hurting and take top if he had won the choice. Spence's sore shoulder was getting worse as the match continued and the first period of action had taken a toll.

Both coaches shout encouragement from the corners of the mat, but neither wrestler even looks in their directions. East Temple fans and Jackson fans are on their feet along with many others in the stadium. Jake toes the line and looks as if he's ready to jump out of his shoes, unable to wait to get back to the action. Spence goes right after him, not backing down in the least. This time it's Jake who locks up a "Russian tie". As Spence squares off and works his counter, Jake pulls then pushes and then with a quick sweep of his leg, trips Spence to the mat and straight to his back. Jake takes advantage and is able hold on to Spence just long enough to get two quick back points. This was a huge 4-point move as Jake takes a 7-3 lead, but Coach Davis' face is expressionless and confident.

"Let's go Spence you gotta get back to work! Score!"

Spence stands to his feet but Jake has his arms around Spence's waist and begins to lift him off the mat. As he brings Spence back to the mat, Spence hits a standing "granby", and rolls across his shoulders and Jake releases him to give up an escape point and maintain a 7-4 lead.

"Go after heeeim Jake get it beaaak"

Jake shoots his "Superduck" move and fakes to the right side and tries to go around Spence on the left side. Spence is ready and backs off with a smile. Spence takes a shot of his own and ends up under Jake and he can feel the set-up the Coach Miles taught him falling into place. Jake pulls him up and Spence steps right across and under Jake's hips and throws an aggressive and unaware Jake Stevens in a hip toss that puts Jake to his back. All the fans collectively gape at the maneuver and the referee slides to the mat to look for Jake's shoulders to touch the mat. For a split second Jake sees the ceiling of the stadium and his eyes wander from the lights to the fans in the upper deck as he struggles to get back to his belly. Spence's shoulder gives him a shot of intense pain and Jake powers himself over to avoid the pin but he's now lost the lead and Spence takes over with score 9-7. Jake works himself to a sitting position for a brief instant and then breaks away from Spence, cutting the lead to 9-8.

For a split second Jake thinks that escape was a little too easy. He takes a quick look at the clock and sees 25 seconds left in the period. Then he looks at Spence and can clearly see pain in his face. Spence backs off and asks for an injury time-out.

Together in their corner, Rudi and Jake watch and Spence and Coach Davis closely.

"Eeeets hees shoulder. Eeets hurting more than we thought. Go after hees shoulder. Tie heem with two on one on his left arm where he ees weak." Apparently, Russian's don't call a "Russian tie" a "Russian tie".

Jake just drinks from a water bottle and keeps an eye on Spence and Coach Davis as Spence squeezes into a thick rubber shoulder brace.

"He should have stuck me just then. He had me."

"Hey! Look at mee! You ween theeese. Hee is hurt. You teaake adveantage!!"

Spence comes back to the circle and the referee

tells him he has 30 seconds of injury time left. If he runs out of injury time and cannot continue, he loses the match. With a nod of the head he walks to the center circle and responds to the ref.

"Let's go."

"Spence, you okay?"

"Just wrestle Stevens, don't worry about me."

Jake stands up out of his stance as if to gather his thoughts and take one extra breath, then he takes a few steps away from the center circle. Jake looks over to Coach Davis and then to Rudi.

"Leeeats go Jake!"

The referee tells Jake to get back to the circle or get hit with a stalling warning. Jake comes back and places his feet on the line. Jake does just what Rudi tells him to do. He takes Spencer's arm in a Russian tie and he can feel Spence's strength wither away. Spence fights back and Jake can hear him grunt in pain. Jake fakes another foot sweep and when Spence shifts his weight, Jake pulls his arm forward to the mat and gets around Spence for 2 points. Jake takes a 10-9 lead and catches Spence's left arm in a "chicken wing" and begins to drive him over to his back. The pressure on Spencer's shoulder is too much to bear and he rolls to his back. The referee gives a count of "one", but before a second count can be made, the clock hits zero. No points are awarded and the score remains 10-9 for Jake Stevens.

Jake has the choice for the final period and Rudi is yelling from the corner to take top.

"Keep heem down and turn heeem."

Spence walks around the outer edge of the mat and tries to move his shoulder and fights the tears that roll off his cheek. Coach Davis takes him to the side and asks if he can continue.

"Well?"

"Well what? It's the finals. It'll hurt for two minutes and I got the rest of my life to heal."

Jake signals to the official that he chooses to take the top position to start the third period. Spence doesn't want to give Jake another chance to work on the shoulder and he explodes off the whistle to get to his feet. Jake picks Spence up and brings him back down to the mat. Spence is moving frantically to get away and tie the match but also to stay one step ahead of Jake and not let him attack the shoulder again. Jake just follows and keeps a hold of Spence, not letting him get away. In the action Jake gets another chicken wing and has Spencer's shoulder again in his grips.

"Turn heem now Jake, turn heem!"

Jake begins to turn Spence to his back and he can sense the pain Spencer is enduring. Jake can see Coach Davis in the corner of his eyes it looks like he's ready to run out to the mat. Just as Jake is about to turn Spence, the chicken wing loosens and Spence is able to roll across his back and go right to his stomach again, no points. Spence groans in pain as he turns and the referee stops the action and calls for another injury time.

"You have thirty seconds left son."

"Okay Spence, after this we've got no more injury time left. You need to get out and win it with a takedown."

Jake stands as Rudi is chirping in his ear, but nothing registers. His eyes are on Spence, Trey and Wes Carlson. As Trey talks to Spence, Assistant Coach Wes Carlson looks straight at Jake with an angry stare. Jake gives back a blank hypnotized gaze. Coach Rudi knows that a victory is in hand but his excitement and words don't penetrate with Jake. Maybe it was Carlson's glare, maybe it was seeing Spence and the Jackson team supporting him, or maybe it was his father watching over him, but he remembered the words Coach gave his team after watching Tony Hardman lose his cool so long ago.

"You don't win anything by wrestling the way Hardman did yesterday. You don't become a winner, you don't become a better wrestler, and you don't become a better man. Hardman lost something within himself yesterday. He lost a little bit of dignity; he lost a bit of his honor. Don't let that happen to you."

At the end of the 30 seconds, Spencer goes to the center circle and gets ready to wrestle. He doesn't look at Jake, he just gets ready. At the whistle Jake stops Spencer's stand up and keeps him down but isn't able to break him down flat. As he listens to Spence struggle and feels his friend weaken underneath him, Jake places both hands on Spencer's back and lets him go with a push in the back. The score is tied at 10 as they both get to their feet and Jake sees the puzzled look in his friend's eyes. Jake walks off the mat with a limp and asks for his own injury time.

"I have a cramp!"

Rudi runs over to him and tells him to sit down so he can stretch the calf. But Jake turns away and waves him away, as if he doesn't want Rudi to touch him. Jake gets back up and limps around the mat, trying to work out the cramp in his calf. In the other corner, Coach Davis tries to tend to Spencer. Rudi catches up to Jake and pulls him to sit on the mat so that his calf can be looked at and stretched. Rudi massages and stretches the leg and Jake begins to nod his head saying that it's feeling better. He stands back up and begins to walk it off.

Jake walks back and forth and he makes his way over to Spencer's corner and as he passes by he gives Coach Davis a sly wink. It turns out that Jake's injury time wasn't for himself, he called it for Spence. Jake was simply faking the cramp and buying time, not for himself, but for his former team mate. With the score tied, and both of the boys wrestling from their feet, the match is as even as it can get. Jake could have probably kept Spence down with the advantage of the bad shoulder, but that doesn't prove who was better this day, just who was hurt this day.

"You guys ready yet?"

Spence shakes his head in amazement.

"Unbelievable, let's wrestle."

The two former teammates walk back to the center together and the crowd rises to their feet. Coach Rudi, too far away to hear what Jake and Spence are communicating about, is just happy that his wrestler is ready to go again.

"What are you doin?" Spence never looks at Jake and keeps moving his shoulder in circles.

"I'm doin what's right. I'm not gonna be the state champ just cuz you're hurtin."

"Okay gentlemen, the score is tied and you have 1 minute 15 left in the third period. Howard, you are out of injury time and Stevens you have one minute left of your injury time."

"Okay, Howard. We're on even ground now. Let's see if you can take me down."

With the extra time to let his shoulder rest, Spencer feels a little stronger. The spasms of pain are gone for the moment. Now that they are wrestling on their feet he can protect his shoulder a little more. With just over a minute left in the match, both Jake and Spencer work to set up their attack. The next takedown will likely win the match and end it. A bad shot can cost them but a perfect set-up can win it all. The last minute becomes a chess match. Since it's tied neither wrestler needs to push the action and risk losing. But as the clock ticks down the action picks up.

Both Jake and Spence want to end it in this final minute. With 40 seconds left Jake makes an attempt and Spencer responds with a quick re-attack. Neither achieves any sort of advantage and the seconds continues to tick by. A takedown wins and Spencer gets in on a double leg attack but Jake kicks his legs back with a hard sprawl. Spencer changes from holding two legs to taking control of one of Jake's legs. As Spence rises to his feet, Jake turns away from Spence with his leg trailing behind him and then tucks his head and does a forward roll, reaching back for one of Spencer's legs. Spence falls forward with the momentum and now each wrestler has one of the other's legs. They battle in the final scramble on the mat that will decide the match.

Jake begins to pick up Spencer's leg and the referee begins to slowly raise his hand and is about to award two points for a takedown and Coach Rudi shouts for a score from the corner. Then, suddenly Spence turns hard and he ends up on top. The referee puts down the hand that was about to rise. Jake hangs on desperately to Spencer's leg that is beginning to slip away. His head is pressed against the mat and Spence can feel his leg beginning to become free. Spencer aches and daggers shoot into his shoulder. Seconds feel like minutes and each effort becomes misery. Jake knows he needs to hang on to that leg or he loses the match but he feels both the leg and his hopes, slipping away.

Spence hangs on to Jakes leg with both arms tight to his chest and tries to squirm his leg free. With the pain growing, he can feel his arm begin to tremble uncontrollably. Spencer lets out a scream of agony and his eyes squeeze tight. Then suddenly he hears the referee yelling out with him.

"Two takedown!"

Jake has lost his grip and score board clicks to 12-10. Jake gets up and Spence immediately lets him go. The clock ticks the final few seconds and the buzzer sounds the end of the match, and the end of a journey. Spencer Howard is a state champion.

Jake buries his head in his hands, but only for a moment. His father taught him to end a match with dignity. As Spencer's hand is raised, Jake walks away, slowly picks up his warm-ups and jogs off, alone.

Coach Davis said that there wasn't any losers in the finals match of a state tournament. That's a hard idea to swallow when you're standing on the second step. After four years of struggle and sacrifice, coming so close but not reaching your goal can leave a bitter taste in your mouth. Jake isn't happy by any means, but he's not bitter. He's disappointed but he's also grateful. He understands the lessons he's been taught and as he stands on the podium he can look back at what he and Spence have accomplished.

When the time comes to receive the medals, Spencer looks out to the crowd from the top step and sees his mother crying. At the end of that letter his father made the promise that he'd be in his corner for each and every one of his matches. Now that his last match has concluded, Spence wonders if his father kept that promise.

# Epilogue

Twenty years later there are many that remember the names, Spencer Howard and Jake Stevens. They may recall watching the finals match. Of those that were there, few will recall the final score and many will not even remember which wrestler actually won the bout. For those involved, the moment will remain in their minds for a lifetime.

Trey Davis retired after taking Jackson to its fourth team state championship. He has retired to his home town of Chicago and spends his days as a frustrated Cubs fan. There are times in the winter when he is drawn back to the sport and will wander into a local high school match.

Coach Rudi brought East Temple to new heights but after his 6th year he moved on to a Division II collegiate program. He still keeps his silver medal on his desk and his wife's picture still sits behind Sergei Belaglosov's.

Wes Carlson became the Head Coach of Jackson High after Coach Davis retired. Jackson H.S. went through a renovation and constructed an new wrestling room. The room was named "Stevens Hall". Wes has a girl and three boys and each of them were coached by Wes at Jackson High. He and Janet are still together.

Tommy Chernich went on to become an All-American in both football and wrestling. He moved to California where he teaches High School Physical Education and coaches both the football and wrestling teams. He doesn't read Spiderman comics any longer but he has the entire library of "The Simpsons" episodes on DVD.

Jake never moved back to Jackson but he visits his father's grave every year before the annual camping trip.

Jake went on to wrestle at the next level but suffered a career ending neck injury that took him off of the competitive mat. He works in the accounting department for a large construction company. He remembers each and every minute of that match with Spence and has never had a single regret. His office is full of pictures of his wrestling memories. He also has a picture of his father hugging him on the mat. Also mounted under the picture in the same frame is his second place state medal. Next to it there is a picture of Spence, Tommy, and himself as teammates in Jackson and then another of the three of them as college team mates in Arizona.

After college, Spence stayed near Jackson and helps out with the local high school team. He owns a restaurant and his employees love him. He runs a flexible schedule that allows every worker some time to be home for their kids. Each year he goes camping with Jake and next week he'll see Wes as his team will face off against Jackson H.S. He and his wife have two sons; his oldest is the 4th ranked 112 pounder in the state. He still keeps that letter his father wrote to him many years ago, and every so often he'll read it to his sons.

Made in the USA
San Bernardino, CA
21 February 2015